MAKING THE GRADE

MAKING THE GRADE

Report of the
Twentieth Century Fund
Task Force on
Federal Elementary and
Secondary Education Policy

Background Paper by
Paul E. Peterson

 The Twentieth Century Fund/New York/1983

The Twentieth Century Fund is an independent research foundation which undertakes policy studies of economic, political, and social institutions and issues. The Fund was founded in 1919 and endowed by Edward A. Filene.

FOREWORD

There are few problems more critical than those facing the nation's public schools. Thus, although education had never been an area of research for the Twentieth Century Fund—many other institutions with greater experience and vastly more resources have been devoted to the field—a few years ago, a small group of Fund Trustees, convinced that the problems of American education are at the heart of many of our economic and social difficulties, urged that we undertake an examination of our schools. Because the Trustees saw the problem as national in scope, they proposed a "national project." After considerable discussion, it was decided that the staff should thoroughly explore what others were doing before considering a possible focus for a study.

And so, more than three years ago, the staff began a reconnaissance that was in itself an education for those involved. What concerned our Trustees, and what the staff recognized very early in its investigation, was the vital necessity of doing a better job of educating young Americans so that they can contribute to and function in contemporary society. This is not to say that all of today's students are less well educated than those of a generation ago. But the exigencies of our fast-changing technological world call for many more skilled young people than ever before in our history, which means increased demands on our schools. The staff found that other institutions were well aware of these demands and that other groups were funding commissions and panels to scrutinize our schools. But no one, it seemed, was looking at what federal policy and federal programs ought to be, and mindful of the strictures of the Trustees, the staff focused on this area.

Paul E. Peterson, a professor of political science and education at the University of Chicago, was asked to prepare a background paper on the

v

federal role in education that could serve as a starting point for an independent Task Force and that would also inform the lay reader. Peterson provided a comprehensive paper, setting forth historical and statistical data and his own conclusions. With it in hand, the Fund then assembled the Task Force. Headed by Robert Wood, former secretary of the Department of Housing and Urban Development, it included a number of authorities with vastly differing perspectives, as well as two Trustees of the Fund who had been in the original group urging that the Fund get involved in education. The Task Force also heard from a number of guest witnesses: Susan Glass, director of public relations, American Federation of Teachers; Sharon Robinson, program director for instruction and professional development, National Education Association; Frank Macchiarola, formerly chancellor, New York City Board of Education; George Hanford, College Board; Gary Sykes, National Institute of Education; and Sar Levitan, George Washington University.

The findings of the Task Force are presented in the Report on the following pages. Given the diverse views of its members, what is surprising is not that they disagreed with Peterson over the condition of public education, and with one another, particularly when it came to the recommendations, which is reflected in specific dissents, but the extent to which they agreed. The members of the Task Force were in accord in their diagnosis and in their policy proposals, which is really remarkable since they did not evade tough and sensitive issues. As an auditor of their deliberations, I must add that they fought hard over their conclusions, thrashing out their differences, refusing to settle for easy compromises. Their meetings were lively and informative, resulting in important and timely proposals.

The Fund is indebted to Bob Wood and his colleagues on the Task Force for carrying out their responsibilities so diligently and so well. We are similarly grateful to Paul Peterson. I also want to express my appreciation to the guests who appeared before the Task Force. And I must make special note of Brewster C. Denny, the vice-chairman of the Fund, and Charles V. Hamilton, the chairman of the Projects Committee, who really initiated this project by prodding the staff and me into taking the risk of entering a new field and for encouraging us to plunge in, immersing ourselves so to speak, rather than tiptoeing in. They are owed special thanks for an exciting and worthwhile experience.

M. J. Rossant, *Director*
THE TWENTIETH CENTURY FUND
May 1983

CONTENTS

LIST OF FIGURES AND TABLES

TASK FORCE MEMBERS

Robert Wood, *chairman*
Henry R. Luce Professor of Democratic Institutions and the Social Order, Wesleyan University; formerly Director of Urban Studies, University of Massachusetts

Brewster C. Denny
Professor of Public Affairs, formerly Dean, Graduate School of Public Affairs, University of Washington

Chester E. Finn, Jr.
Codirector and Professor of Education and Public Policy, Center on Education Policy, Institute for Public Policy Studies, Vanderbilt University

Patricia Albjerg Graham
Dean and Charles Warren Professor of the History of Education, Graduate School of Education, Harvard University

Charles V. Hamilton
Wallace S. Sayre Professor of Government, Department of Political Science, Columbia University

Carlos R. Hortas
Chairman, Department of Romance Languages, Hunter College

Diane Ravitch
Adjunct Associate Professor, Teachers College, Columbia University

Wilson Riles
Wilson Riles & Associates, Sacramento; formerly Superintendent of Public Instruction and Director of Education, State Department of Education, Sacramento

Donald M. Stewart
President, Spelman College, Atlanta

Robert E. Wentz
Superintendent, Clark County School District, Las Vegas

Rosalyn Yalow
Chairman, Department of Clinical Science, Montefiore Medical Center, New York

Rapporteur:
Paul E. Peterson
Professor of Political Science and Education, Department of Political Science, University of Chicago

Report of the Task Force

The nation's public schools are in trouble. By almost every measure—the commitment and competency of teachers, student test scores, truancy and dropout rates, crimes of violence—the performance of our schools falls far short of expectations. To be sure, there are individual schools and school districts with devoted teachers doing a commendable job of educating their students, but too many young people are leaving the schools without acquiring essential learning skills and without self-discipline or purpose. The problem we face was succinctly summed up just three years ago by the President's Commission for a National Agenda for the Eighties when it reported that

> . . . continued failure by the schools to perform their traditional role adequately, together with a failure to respond to the emerging needs of the 1980s, may have disastrous consequences for this nation.*

This Task Force believes that this threatened disaster can be averted only if there is a national commitment to excellence in our public schools. While we strongly favor maintaining the diversity in educational practices that results from the decentralization of the schools, we think that schools across the nation must at a minimum provide the same core components to all students. These components are the basic skills of reading, writing, and calculating; technical capability in computers; training in science and foreign languages; and knowledge of civics, or what Aristotle called the education of the citizenry in the spirit of the polity.

As we see it, the public schools, which constitute the nation's most important institution for the shaping of future citizens, must go further. We think that they should ensure the availability of large numbers of skilled and capable individuals without whom we cannot sustain a complex and competitive economy. They should foster understand-

---

*President's Commission for a National Agenda for the Eighties, *A National Agenda for the Eighties* (Washington, D.C.: U.S. Government Printing Office, 1980).

3

ing, discipline, and discernment, those qualities of mind and temperament that are the hallmarks of a civilized polity and that are essential for the maintenance of domestic tranquility in a polyethnic constitutional democracy. And they should impart to present and future generations a desire to acquire knowledge, ranging from the principles of science to the accumulated wisdom and shared values that derive from the nation's rich and varied cultural heritage.

These are admittedly formidable tasks that too few schools today come close to accomplishing. The Task Force believes that the schools must make a concerted effort to improve their performance and that there is a clear national interest in helping schools everywhere to do so. That interest can be asserted and dramatized most effectively by the federal government. The federal government, after all, is charged with providing for the security and well-being of our democratic society, which rest largely on a strong and competent system of public education. It is in the best position to focus public attention on the vital importance of quality in our schools and to support its attainment. The federal government should be able to foster excellence in education, serving as a firm but gentle goad to states and local communities without impeding or restricting state and local control of and accountability for the schools.

Excessive Burdens

Before putting forward our proposals for a new federal policy on elementary and secondary schooling, we think it useful to identify what has gone wrong. Why, despite spending more per student than every other advanced nation, is there a growing gap between the goals and achievements of our schools? Many developments—economic, demographic, social, political—have contributed, directly and indirectly. We have always demanded a great deal of our schools, but never before have we demanded of them as much as we have over the past thirty years. On one hand we have charged them with being the melting pot, the crucible for dissolving racial divisiveness, and on the other for sustaining, and even exalting, ethnic distinctiveness.

The schools, moreover, have had to provide a wide array of social services, acting as surrogate parent, nurse, nutritionist, sex counselor, and policeman. At the same time, they are charged with training increasing percentages of the nation's youth, including large numbers of hard-to-educate youngsters, to improved levels of competency so that they can effectively enter a labor market in which employers are currently demanding both technical capability and the capacity to learn new skills. In essence, the skills that were once possessed by only a few must now be held by the many if the United States is to remain competitive in an advancing technological world.

Demographic changes as well as changes in attitudes toward traditional mores and values have also had a marked influence. The schools have had to cope with more children, and especially more problem children, than ever before—those who are without the rudiments of English and those who are unmotivated or prone to violence, quite apart from those who are physically handicapped. Problems have also come about as a result of the ready availability of drugs, the growing number of family breakups and the increased permissiveness in those remaining intact, the distractions of television and of easily affordable video games, the growth of underworld culture.

The difficulties of coping with these burdens have been compounded in some cities by inappropriate judicial intervention and by the spread of the trade-union mentality that has accompanied the bureaucratization and politicization of the schools. As a consequence, already large administrative staffs have burgeoned, and new rules and procedures have been promulgated, forcing classroom teachers to spend more time on paperwork and less on teaching. The rise in teacher and administrative unions has thus helped transform what had been a noble though poorly compensated profession into a craft led by collective bargaining organizations with a focus on bread-and-butter issues—wages, working conditions, and job security (for which read seniority).

The federal courts have been particularly criticized for playing so conspicuous a role. There is no doubt that they were active in enforcing the rights guaranteed by the Fourteenth Amendment, and that their activity was critical to ensuring those rights for many citizens. But the spectacle of judges, who had little knowledge—and no experience—of the intricacies of operating school systems, taking over responsibility was often harmful. More often than not, though, judges had no choice. They acted because politicians in state legislatures and Congress, in state houses and the White House, failed to act. In most jurisdictions no local political leadership emerged; cowardice rather than courage prevailed, creating a leadership vacuum that the courts filled.

The Federal Presence

In recent years the federal executive and legislative branches have enlarged their roles. In the view of some critics, federal intervention looms so large that it has not only overstepped constitutional limitations but bears responsibility for most of the failings of the schools. We consider these criticisms exaggerated. True, since 1965, with the passage of the Elementary and Secondary Education Act (ESEA), the executive branch has intervened, by law and by regulation, in many school activities, tilting the allocation of resources to compensatory education and affirmative action programs. But the achievements of some federal activities must be acknowledged. Its Title I program as well as Head

Start have been particularly successful, especially among children in elementary schools where these programs were concentrated. Even affirmative action programs registered some success, although most were hampered by excessive federal manipulation. Federal involvement was underscored by the establishment of the U.S. Department of Education in 1979–80, but long before it was on the scene some observers claimed that the delicate balance of what had been a complicated but relatively efficient educational system had been needlessly upset by the federal presence.

Many other criticisms of the federal role in elementary and secondary education are warranted, but not the complaint that the federal government has violated its constitutional authority. This Task Force believes that educating the young is a compelling national interest, and that action by the federal government can be as appropriate as action by state and local governments. Certainly, federal intervention was not only appropriate but necessary in bringing about desegregation of the public schools, and in providing needed assistance to poor and handicapped children.

All too often, though, the nature of federal intervention has been counterproductive, entailing heavy costs and undesirable consequences. Direct federal outlays accounted, at their peak, for less than 10 percent of total annual spending on the schools, but by resorting to compulsory regulation and mandated programs, the federal government has swelled school bureaucracies, imposed dubious and expensive procedures, and forced state and local governments to reallocate substantial portions of their scarce revenues. What is more, its emphasis on promoting equality of opportunity in the public schools has meant a slighting of its commitment to educational quality.* Thus, the federal government has not only had a pervasive influence on the spending of local school districts but has undoubtedly played a part in many of the other troubles of the schools.**

Despite all of its shortcomings, however, there is a need for a continued federal role, in part because equality and excellence are not mutually exclusive objectives. We think that both objectives should be

---

Comment by Mr. Riles: The "slighting of its commitment to educational quality" by the federal government should not be blamed on the promotion of equality of opportunity. As previously stated in this report, Congress has historically "refrained" from addressing the issues of educational quality. I believe it is essential that both issues be addressed.

**Comment by Ms. Graham:* There have been many mistakes in federal education programs, much misplaced money, numerous stupidities. None should be justified. There have also been important achievements, particularly for children from low-income families through Title I of the Elementary and Secondary Education Act, through Head Start, and for young minority children in the

vigorously pursued through a fresh approach, one that reflects the national concern for a better-educated America and that strikes a reasonable and effective balance between quality and equality. The federal government must continue to help meet the special needs of poor and minority students while taking the lead in meeting the general and overwhelming need for educational quality. Federal education policy must function, moreover, in ways that complement rather than weaken local control. This calls for a change in direction, replacing the current emphasis on regulations and mandates with a new emphasis on incentives.

The Federal Commitment

Even before there were public schools everywhere, the federal government expressed its commitment to education. The Northwest Ordinance of 1787 specified that land was to be set aside for education purposes in every town and rural area. In the words of the proviso to the ordinance, "Religion, morality, and knowledge being necessary to good government and the happiness of mankind, schools and the means of education shall forever be encouraged." Thus, soon after the nation's founding, its leaders recognized that the experiment in political democracy upon which they were embarking could not succeed without an educated citizenry.

Seventy-five years later, in the midst of the Civil War, Congress sought to enlist the aid of the nation's educational institutions in the Morrill Act, which granted land for the purpose of supporting colleges of agriculture and mechanical arts. In this century, Congress passed the Smith-Hughes Act, which provided federal support for vocational education, and the National Defense Education Act (NDEA), which, in the immediate aftermath of the Soviet Union's Sputnik, called for improved training in such critical subject areas as science, mathematics, and foreign languages.

Although Congress has from time to time acknowledged the essential need for public education and even for specific kinds of education, it has refrained, apparently deliberately, from addressing the issue of

---

(Continued from page 4)
South (especially areas affected by the 1954 *Brown v. Board of Education* desegregation decision). Both the mistakes and achievements are worthy of note. Given the conflicting mandates the public schools have been assigned, the tone of this document is more critical of their performance than I believe justified either by the evidence presented here or from other sources with which I am familiar.

Messrs. Hortas and Wentz wish to associate themselves with Ms. Graham's comment.

educational quality. This matter, with good reason, was left to the discretion of the states and localities. The control of public education, even though subject to constitutional restriction, is exercised by thousands of school boards and school superintendents within a legal framework set up by fifty different state legislatures. There has been no one place—and we do not think there should be—in which a national policy defines the correct school curriculum or the proper qualifications for teachers, or sets forth the precise duration of the school day or year. These are matters that traditionally have been left to lay citizens, reinforced by the advice and counsel of professional educators or schools of education. We believe it should remain that way.

The genius of our decentralized arrangements is that we have managed to forge a national education system that allows room for variations and even for disagreements. This is not to say that the Task Force is satisfied with the performance of local school districts. To the contrary, we believe that the vast majority must do much better. But because learning depends upon intangibles—the leadership provided by a school principal, the chemistry between teachers and students, the extent of parental involvement and support—we strongly favor leaving control over schooling at the local level. Good schools cannot be created by federal mandate. They grow from the ground up in complex and often idiosyncratic fashion. Most good schools have many characteristics in common, but there is no formula that can bring about their duplication because there is no one best way of providing a first-rate education.

Quality of Leadership

Because quality in education is easier to recognize than to define, some of the reluctance of Congress to face up to the issue is understandable. Educational quality cannot be legislated into existence. Still, Congress must not continue to be ostrichlike about the failings of primary and secondary school education. Its readiness to legislate on other aspects of education, whether in programs for the handicapped, or for all those whose English is limited or nonexistent, or for special interests—for example, the National Educational Association—that successfully lobbied for the establishment of the Department of Education while ignoring declines in test scores, suggests to many Americans that quality in education is not a national goal. That false impression must be erased.

This Task Force calls on the executive and legislative branches of the federal government to emphasize the need for better schools and a better education for all young Americans. We have singled out a number of specific areas in which the federal government, mainly through a series of incentives, can act to improve the quality of education in the public schools. Most of our proposals are directed toward improving the quality of teaching, ensuring proficiency in English while developing fluency in foreign languages, and promoting ways to increase proficiency in mathematics and science. We then go on to discuss the nature and content of the federal role in education, what it can do to further quality as well as equality in schooling, and the extent of choice that ought to be made available to parents.

Quality of Teachers

The traditional commitment of teachers to quality education has been challenged by many forces, some that have affected all of society, others that are peculiar to the community of educators. The teacher—along with all other authority figures—does not appear to command the respect commonly accorded a generation ago. The complex organizational structure in which the classroom teacher now operates restricts independence and autonomy; as new organizational positions have proliferated, many of the best teachers have been "promoted" to better paying administrative positions, devaluing the status of the teacher. In addition, the organizations—the unions and professional associations—to which teachers belong have protected their weakest members rather than winning rewards for their strongest. They have promoted the principle of equal pay or, at best, a differential pay scale that primarily takes into account educational background and seniority, thereby limiting the financial incentives available for rewarding superior professional work. The collective bargaining process, moreover, has not only made it difficult to encourage promising teachers or dismiss poor ones, it has forced many of the best to leave teaching for more financially rewarding work. The result is that the quality of teaching suffers.

Deterioration in quality is probably greatest in specialized subjects, most markedly in mathematics and science. Because of the constant need of industry for skilled personnel, teachers in these fields can easily find more profitable employment. This problem is not new, of course, but standardized salary schedules, reinforced by the collective bargaining process, have made for staff shortages in mathematics and science in many local school districts. School boards frequently resort to such stratagems as paying science and mathematics teachers overtime for extra work instead of directly facing up to the unions and to the need to increase salaries for specialized teachers in short supply.

Because the institutional arrangements and procedures governing teachers are so well entrenched, incremental changes in federal policy cannot by themselves dramatically improve the quality of instruction. The Task Force is convinced that what is required is a major federal initiative that unmistakably emphasizes the critical importance of quality teachers in our schools. *We propose the establishment of a national Master Teachers Program, funded by the federal government, that recognizes and rewards teaching excellence.*

Under our proposed program, the best teachers from every state would be awarded the accolade of Master Teacher and a monetary grant—say, $40,000 a year—above that of the ceiling for teachers' salaries for a period of five years. Criteria for selection might be set by such established agencies as the National Endowment for the Humanities, the National Science Foundation, and other federal agencies, with the actual selections made by them after their canvassing of local advisers, including school boards and school administrators, teachers, and parents.

In maintaining Master Teachers in the program for five years, we propose that up to one full year should be devoted to professional improvement through graduate or similar work, and that additional funds, for tuition or for the assistance of graduate students, should be made available for such purposes. The remaining four years would be spent teaching, with perhaps some of that time used to work with and provide help to other teachers.*

Rather than spell out the details of the proposed program, we have set down the guidelines we think should be followed. We recommend the adoption of an incentive approach, establishing clear criteria for teachers of exceptional merit and making the awards numerous enough to attract national attention and substantial enough for long enough to keep Master Teachers in the classroom.

It is our view that the proposed program would help pave the way for reconsideration of merit-based personnel systems for teachers, which we believe would foster improvements in quality. Despite many surveys of public servants and professionals that have disclosed a strong preference for merit pay increases and promotions, school boards and legislators have almost always yielded to union demands for equal pay. Collective bargaining has served teachers and the public by improving working conditions and compensation, and we do not want to see it abandoned. But both the public and teachers would be even better served if the opposing sides in the bargaining process—the unions and local school boards—realized that merit-based systems and collective bargaining are not incompatible.

Dissent by Ms. Yalow: I oppose the establishment of a Master Teachers Program. It would be expensive and would not address a real need, namely the shortage of teachers in chemistry, physics, and mathematics. I believe it would hurt morale in that a reward for a limited period to be followed by a period of reduced salary would be a retrogressive step. Moreover, I question whether it is necessary or desirable to give a "Master Teacher" a full year for "professional improvement." What is required is a salary structure that reflects competency and that would aid in recruitment of teachers in short supply. The goals of the proposed Master Teachers Program seem noble, but the mechanism suggested is highly unlikely to have the desired effect.

The Master Teachers Program will be expensive—just how expensive will depend on the number of awards made each year. At a minimum there should be at least one award for each congressional district, but we think that many more should be given. By the fifth year of the program, the cost could run as high as $5 billion.

The Task Force believes that such an expense is warranted. Good teachers are as valuable to the nation as new tanks or fighter planes or a new highway. By making so visible and costly a commitment, the federal government will not only be assuming leadership in the quest for educational excellence but undertaking a major program to help achieve it.

The Primacy of English

Our political democracy rests on the conviction that each citizen should have the capacity to participate fully in our political life; to read newspapers, magazines, and books; to bring a critical intelligence to television and radio; to be capable of resisting emotional manipulation and of setting events within their historical perspective; to express ideas and opinions about public affairs; and to vote thoughtfully—all activities that call for literacy in English. Accordingly, *the Task Force recommends that the federal government clearly state that the most important objective of elementary and secondary education in the United States is the development of literacy in the English language.*

A significant number of young Americans come from homes where English is not the first language, and many now live in neighborhoods in an increasing number of states in which languages other than English are spoken. Although this nation has become more aware of the value of ethnic identities than it was during previous influxes of non-English-speaking immigrants, anyone living in the United States who is unable to speak English cannot fully participate in our society, its culture, its politics. This is not because of prejudice but because most Americans speak, write, and think in English. English is, after all, our national language.

We recommend, then, that students in elementary school learn to read, write, speak, and listen in English. As children advance in grade, these skills should be continually improved. By the time they finish high school, students ought to possess such advanced cognitive skills as reasoning, critical analysis, the ability to explain and understand complex ideas, and to write clearly and correctly.

Many different methods have been proposed for educating children who are not literate in English. It is not the role of the Task Force nor is it the responsibility of the federal government to instruct our schools and teachers on which pedagogy is most appropriate. The federal role, we believe, is to guarantee that all children have equal educational opportunity. Therefore, *the Task Force recommends that federal funds now going to bilingual programs be used to teach non-English-speaking children how to speak, read, and write English.** Local school districts may decide to teach children in more than one language or to teach them a language other than English. Although we believe that the failure to recognize the primacy of English is a grave error, that is their prerogative. The distinctive nature of the federal role, we believe, derives from the premise that all of us must be able to communicate with one another as fellow citizens.

Accordingly, *the Task Force recommends that the federal government promote and support proficiency in English for all children in the public schools, but especially for those who do not speak English, or have only limited command of it.*

At the same time, the Task Force considers the ability to speak and read a second language a valuable resource for both the individual and the nation. Acquiring facility in a foreign language can help to improve a student's understanding and command of English, and lead to the appreciation of the literature and culture of another people, which is clearly educationally desirable. It should also be an advantage in a business or professional career.

From a national perspective, young men and women with proficiency in foreign languages are sorely needed now that we are increasingly involved in competitive trade and investment with the rest of the world. More and more jobs will be available in government, industry, trade, commerce, and the universities for Americans who can converse with other people in their own languages, and who can participate in strengthening our international ties.

This Task Force wants every American public school student to have the opportunity to acquire proficiency in a second language. Unfortunately, there is no practical possibility of obtaining this objective quickly. The neglect of foreign language study and instruction in the United States is of such long standing that we simply do not have enough language teachers to provide adequate training. Nevertheless, we propose that proficiency in a second language should be a long-term

---

Dissent by Mr. Hortas: It is unquestionable that all students must learn to speak, read, and write English in order to function in our society. Nonetheless, bilingual programs in which children are taught in English and in their native language are essential if we are to provide a healthy learning environment for children of limited English ability. Because local school districts cannot afford to underwrite such programs, I recommend that the proposal on federal impact aid, set forth later in this report, be applied to bilingual programs. The academic achievements of children of limited English-speaking ability will be significantly greater if the child's first language skills are maintained and improved.

goal. We must begin a training program now if we are to achieve that goal in future decades.* The federal government can help in the training of language teachers and in encouraging and assisting in programs for students with proficiency in English to learn a second language that may or may not be a language spoken in their homes.

Our aim is to see this second-language policy sponsored by the federal government and carried out by state and local governments. The immediate need is for a modest matching grant program to train language teachers. Even though it will take time and effort, we think that a comprehensive approach to the study of languages, in which fluency in English is primary but adequate training in a second language is also made available, is absolutely essential if the United States is to be a leader among nations in the next century.**

Comment by Mr. Hortas: Every public school student should start the study of a foreign language in elementary school, which is standard educational practice in the developed countries of the world. A knowledge of a second language at an early age will stimulate a better appreciation of our country's cultural pluralism. The achievement of proficiency in a second language must be a project for this decade, not for future generations.

Ms. Graham and Mr. Denny wish to associate themselves with Mr. Hortas's comment.

**Comment by Ms. Yalow:* I am in complete agreement with the Task Force recommendation about the essentiality of all Americans acquiring proficiency in English. In addition, it is desirable to develop a cadre with proficiency in foreign languages. Therefore, I accept that every American public school student should have the opportunity to acquire proficiency in a foreign language. But I really doubt the desirability of recommending that all high school students be required to study a foreign language. Is such competency really necessary for a farmer in Iowa, a coal miner in West Virginia, or a factory worker in the textile mills of the South? It might be highly desirable for a shopkeeper or a secretary in a bilingual community. The extent of competency, whether it should be ability to read, write, or speak fluently, should depend on personal and professional interests.

If there appears to be a severe shortage of foreign language teachers at present, perhaps this shortage would more easily be remedied by taking advantage of the large number of people in our country for whom English is not the first language and who have sufficient fluency in both English and the foreign language to be ideal as teachers. Often they do not have appropriate education courses or the right degrees. It is perhaps heretical to suggest that the education courses or degrees are not essential for teaching students to develop proficiency in a foreign language. Teachers without the right credentials but with competency in the foreign language and English could be employed on an adjunct basis if there are rules against their serving as regular teachers.

Mr. Wentz wishes to associate himself with Ms. Yalow's comment.

In the long run, these recommendations to ensure fluency in English are the only kind that make sense. The nation cannot afford a multiplicity of special language programs in every community in which ethnolinguistic minorities are present in significant numbers. More important, school children to whom English is an alien language are being cheated if it remains unfamiliar to them; they will never swim in the American mainstream unless they are fluent in English. The best way to ensure the nation's linguistic resources is to make literacy in English the primary objective and to promote literacy in a second language as a valuable supplement to, not a substitute for, English.*

Science and Mathematics

At the turn of the twentieth century, there was no real need for widespread scientific literacy. Today, training in mathematics and science is critical to our economy. Our citizens must be educated in science if they are to participate intelligently in political decisions about such controversial issues as radiation, pollution, and nuclear energy. *The Task Force recommends that the federal government emphasize programs to develop basic scientific literacy among all citizens and to provide advanced training in science and mathematics for secondary school students.*

The schools must go beyond the teaching of basic science to give adequate training in advanced science and mathematics to a large enough number of students to ensure that there are ample numbers capable of filling the increasing number of jobs demanding these skills. The Reagan administration has proposed a $50 million scholarship program for students in mathematics and science, which we think is a step in the right direction. The more ambitious programs emerging from Congress move even further in that direction. Our preference is for an incentive program to augment the supply of teachers in science and mathematics as well as in foreign languages. Federal loans might be made available to prospective teachers who exhibit exceptional skills and who are pursuing degree programs in areas of existing or anticipated shortages. Those who complete their educational programs might be forgiven up to 10 percent of the funds lent to them for every year of classroom teaching—for a maximum of five years.

Comment by Mr. Hortas: No bilingual program in the United States promotes another language as a *substitute for English*. In fact, intensive English instruction is a part of every bilingual program. Bilingual programs attempt to show that English is not, in and of itself, a superior or richer language than the student's native language. There is a greater social benefit in promoting and encouraging linguistic diversity than in calling for specious uniformity.

Better Education for All

In proposing new federal measures to stimulate national interest in improving the quality of public education, we urge that they not come at the expense of children from low-income families or of children suffering from one or another disability. In recent years the federal education effort has concentrated on the needs of special categories of students—those from low-income homes, the handicapped, the non-English speaking—because states and local governments failed to meet national educational objectives for them. By furnishing special services to the handicapped and by addressing the educational needs of the poor, the federal role has had much the same influence as it had in desegregating the schools. Without such intervention, many states and most local school boards would not have done what clearly needed doing.

But if categorical programs have their uses, critics argue that there are not only too many of them but that many of these proliferating programs are poorly designed. They go on to argue that, while minorities may not have been effectively organized at state and local levels to secure needed programs two decades ago, the political organization and sophistication of such groups has so increased—in part because of federal assistance—that they no longer need the extensive federal protection that they once did. Although this may be the case in many large cities, the political power of minorities is far less potent in most school districts.

Perhaps the most persuasive reason for federal support of categorical programs is that, even under favorable political conditions, few local school systems have the will to concentrate their resources on the minority of students with special needs. Moreover, recent political and economic conditions have been anything but favorable for local governments. The cost of educating children with special needs has forced many school districts to resort to imposing taxes on productive members of the community without providing immediate benefits in return. Business firms along with residents in higher income brackets may choose to leave communities where the tax burden for educating the children of poor, needy residents is relatively heavy. Accordingly, *the Task Force supports continuing federal efforts to provide special educational programs for the poor—and for the handicapped.*

We applaud the steps taken by Congress to simplify regulatory restrictions and to reduce the overlap among many programs. In enacting legislation acknowledging the responsibility of the federal government for groups with special needs, *the Task Force believes that the guiding principle should be that categorical programs required by the federal government should be paid for from the federal treasury.* These categorical programs are not special-interest legislation serving particular groups at the expense of the nation as a whole. To the contrary, compensatory programs and education for the handicapped concentrate limited resources on specific populations and in particular areas where the need for better education is especially urgent, thereby providing the equality of opportunity essential for the well-being of our democracy. Their cost, then, should be assumed by the federal government, not by states or localities, although local school districts must take the responsibility for the effective provision of special help.

The Task Force also recommends that "impact" aid, originally aimed at helping cushion the burden imposed on local school facilities by the children of military personnel, be reformulated to focus on school districts that are overburdened by substantial numbers of immigrant children. During World War II, the influx of the military into particular communities placed unusual burdens on local school districts; currently, when cities and regions compete vigorously for defense spending, the military is often a boon to local economies. Under today's conditions, we believe it fitting that federal impact aid should be used when large numbers of aliens and immigrants, many of whom are poor, place a special burden on local school districts. Given the Supreme Court decision reaffirming the right of children of illegal aliens to equal educational opportunities, the federal government has an obligation to temporarily assist states and localities facing added costs for educating these children, who usually need special help.

A related problem is the plight of localities in economic distress—mainly in the nation's central cities but also in impoverished rural areas, where there is an undue concentration of low-income groups, where high unemployment persists, and where there is a clear and urgent need for better education of the young. *The Task Force thus urges that federal attention and assistance go to depressed localities that have concentrations of immigrant and/or impoverished groups as well as those that are already making strong efforts to improve their education performance.* Quantitative measures of needs are available, grants can be flexible, and targets can be specific.

Educational Research

Proponents of the cabinet-level Department of Education predicted that its establishment would provide federal leadership for the public schools. Since it was set up, that prophecy has not been fulfilled, partly because initially the department had to take responsibility for a set of questionable and intrusive policies, partly because its role was downgraded with the change of administrations. This Task Force did not spend much time examining the function and performance of the Department of Education. Some members took the position that it was largely irrelevant; others thought that it would be better to restore it to a restructured Department of Health and Human Services, which might give it a stronger political influence; still others believed that its activities should be split up among various federal agencies.

But in the course of our deliberations, we had many opportunities to appreciate the value of the department's information and analysis on the state of our public schools. It does not seem necessary to keep the Department of Education in being simply because it has responsibility for information gathering and research, but federal responsibility for those activities ought to be maintained. Federal agencies have long had experience in the field and are superbly situated for collating data from the states. Whatever the fate of the department, we urge that the collection of data remain a federal responsibility.

Ever since it was established in 1867, the federal Office (now Department) of Education has gathered such basic data as the average number of pupils in daily attendance in the nation's schools, the number of teachers and other school employees, and the cost of educational services. More recently, the federal government has undertaken broad surveys of school practices, pupil performance, and the consequences of schooling for adult life. It has also funded the development of new curricula, studies of the effects of various educational innovations, and basic research on the processes of human learning. Currently, two agencies of the Department of Education bear much of this responsibility for research—the National Center for Education Statistics gathers information and data, and the National Institute of Education supports research and development. (Other federal agencies, such as the Census Bureau and the National Science Foundation, along with private foundations, also sponsor education research.) The results of data collection and research have proven useful in identifying areas of progress or emerging difficulties; sometimes they have pointed toward possible solutions; and sometimes they have served to focus the national debate on the schools.

Research on questions of educational quality can have symbolic as well as substantive value. For example, the study of the effects of school segregation undertaken by James Coleman for the Office of Education in 1965 focused public attention on the perniciousness of racism. Subsequent studies stimulated and informed public debate over such critical questions as the effects of school desegregation on "white flight," the results of compensatory education programs, and the relative merits of public and private schools. Current national concern with the quality of public education, particularly at the high school level, has been stimulated in part by findings of such federally sponsored projects as the National Assessment of Educational Progress.

The Task Force recommends federal support for a number of specific activities:

- The collection of factual information about various aspects of the education system itself. Such data gathering is traditional, uncontroversial, and essential if policies are to be developed on the basis of accurate information. Because collecting this information seems so routine, and because it has no particular "constituency," it is often starved for resources and is always vulnerable to the government's periodic efforts to "reduce paperwork." We urge that collection of this information be made mandatory.

• The collection of information about the educational performance of students, teachers, and schools across the nation. Although the National Assessment of Educational Progress has done useful work, and should be continued and strengthened, current federal efforts to appraise the quality of American education are inadequate. We urge the federal government, for example, to collect and disseminate information available from routine tests. Nearly every elementary school student regularly takes tests of performance and achievement in various skills and subjects, many of them prepared by private agencies and administered by school systems. The majority of states require high school students to take "competency" tests; college-bound students take a battery of tests developed by the Educational Testing Service and the American College Testing Service. All of this data should be collected and made accessible to researchers.

Other information would be useful too. In addition to knowing how many high school juniors are "taking mathematics," for example, it would be enlightening to know how many years of mathematics they have previously taken, what their courses have covered, and what kind of training and qualifications their teachers possess.

• Evaluation of federally sponsored education programs. Most federal education programs have some form of built-in evaluation, but all too often these are superficial, self-serving, or (especially when the results are critical) not readily accessible. A good rule of thumb, the Task Force believes, is that whenever the federal government conducts an educational program, whether it is a simple transfer of resources to college students or an attempt to foster a major pedagogical change in elementary schools, a "report card" on the effectiveness of that program should be made public.

• Fundamental research into the learning process. The more that is known about how youngsters learn, the better they can be taught. Learning is an immensely complicated affair, and progress has been made on it in recent years, partly with federal support. But the federal government spends a pittance on such research compared with its support for basic research into health, agriculture, the physical sciences, and weaponry. More money is needed, enough to enlist able scholars in the process—as designers of research agendas, as researchers, as "peer reviewers" of research proposals, and as evaluators of research findings.

Unfortunately, the National Institute of Education and other federal agencies have too often allowed their interests and resources to be diverted into peripheral topics, into fruitless quests for "quick fixes," or into catering to particular educational interest groups. So if the federal government is to be given primary responsibility for educational research, it must adopt sensible ground rules and safeguards to assure that its research is sound and comprehensive, and it must be supported in these efforts through the political process.

Provision of Choice

Although elementary and, to a considerable extent, secondary education in the United States is compulsory, it does not have to be public school education. American parents, who traditionally have insisted on a say in their children's schooling, can turn to private schools when they are not satisfied with public schooling—and some 10 percent of the school-age population attends private schools today. But the vast majority of children attend public schools, and it is critical that their parents be able to influence the quality of schooling.

Public schools are governed by local school boards, whose members in most districts are elected and are generally responsive to the parent-teacher associations (PTAs) whose members helped elect them. In many districts, PTAs or comparable parent groups play a constructive role, raising extra money for the schools and building community support for them. That role is a rarity in many urban districts, where community spirit is often lacking and where local schools are subject to the directives of higher authorities, who are frequently insensitive to community concerns.

The major choice available to parents opting for the public school system is their selection of a community in which to live. In large metropolitan areas subdivided into numerous small- to medium-sized suburbs, parents have a great deal of choice among many different—and different quality—public schools. A significant measure of the market value of a house is the prevailing opinion on the quality of the schools where it is located.

The biggest drawback to these options is the cost to the family. To send a child to a good public school often means paying more for a house or apartment. Private school tuition is extremely costly and must be paid over and above the taxes paid for local public schools. Family income thus limits choice. Only 4.8 percent of the nonpublic elementary school population came from families with incomes of less than $5,000 a year, compared with the 13.2 percent of the public school population. At the other end of the scale, 18.2 percent of elementary nonpublic school pupils came from families with incomes of $25,000 or more, compared with only 8.9 percent of public school pupils.

Many proposals have been made in recent years to give parents more of a voice in choosing where their children are educated. Among them are tax credit plans and tuition vouchers. The Task Force does not endorse such proposals or recommend a major redefinition of the relationship between public and nonpublic schools. We believe that the provision of free public education must continue to be a public responsibility of high priority, while support of nonpublic education should remain a private obligation. Yet we recognize that some children have not been able to learn in the present setting of public education. We cannot ignore, for example, students who repeatedly fail city or state competency examinations or fail in other ways to attain their academic capacity. Rather than having such students either held back time and time again or promoted year after year to new levels of remediation, *the Task Force recommends the establishment of special federal fellowships for them, which would be awarded to school districts to encourage the creation of small, individualized programs staffed by certified teachers and run as small-scale academies.* Eligibility for these fellowships, available to no more than 5 percent of public school enrollment, should be jointly determined by local, state, and federal school officials. Such an experiment, designed to benefit those who have been unable to learn in public schools, might provide the intensive and encouraging environment that these students need, and would free up the substantial resources now being spent on remediation with so little to show for it.**

Comment by Mr. Denny: I fully support the position taken by the Task Force on the provision of choice and our position not to support such ideas as tax credit plans and tuition vouchers. I also support the recommendation for the establishment of special federal fellowships for students who cannot learn in the present setting of public education. But I would also like such a fellowship program to offer support for especially able students who live in school districts where quality educational opportunities do not exist in the public schools. Such a program should follow the recommendation of the Task Force in providing fellowships to public school districts to encourage the creation of programs staffed by certified teachers and run as small-scale academies.

**Comment by Ms. Graham*:   Although I agree with this proposal because it has much potential merit, I want to point out the danger that such a program could lead to resegregation without significant remediation.

Comment by Mr. Finn: This fellowship proposal is a variation on the idea that has sometimes been called "literary vouchers," an idea that I find interesting and potentially worthwhile for those youngsters having the least success in ordi-

Leadership in Education

While the federal role in promoting equality of opportunity and educational quality in the nation's schools is significant, elementary and secondary education in the United States must primarily remain a responsibility of state and local governments. A state-supported, locally administered system of public schools has successfully survived numerous challenges for more than one hundred years. By and large, this decentralized system of education has served more pupils, has provided a broader range of services, has proved more flexible in response to changing conditions, and has moderated class and group antagonisms more successfully than have the school systems of most other industrial nations.

But even though state and local governments should continue to bear the major responsibility for the provision of educational services, it is increasingly important that the federal government emphasize the pressing need for a high-quality system of education open to all Americans, regardless of race or economic position. Toward this end, the

---

(Continued from page 18)

nary public schools. As formulated by the Task Force, however, it makes little or no use of the remarkable educational resource already present in some 18,000 private schools in the United States. Moreover, it cannot fairly be regarded as a substitute for or an alternative to various plans that have been advanced to assist those who would like to send their children to private schools but cannot afford to do so. While welcoming the Task Force's general endorsement of the principle of educational choice, I deeply regret the unwillingness of my colleagues to regard the nongovernmental schools already attended by one child in ten as a full and legitimate element of the nation's educational enterprise and as a particularly important resource in achieving the Task Force's vigorously stated goal of improved educational quality.

Comment by Ms. Yalow: I do not support a fellowship or tuition scholarship program for either the gifted or educationally retarded student. There are few schools or school districts, particularly in urban or suburban regions, which are so small as to make impracticable the setting aside of special classes for each of these groups. I believe the mixing in the same class of students with vastly differing abilities in the name of equality has been a retrogressive step. All students cannot learn at the same rate or acquire the same degree of competency. There is no a priori reason why a public school cannot provide a learning environment equal to that of a private school. Segregation according to ability as previously was done would assure each child an opportunity to develop in accordance with that ability. The fact that parents are turning to private schools is a measure of the inadequacy of public schools. Any available funding should go to support of special programs in the public school system and not to removing students from that system.

Task Force has put forward a coordinated policy of overall federal support for American schools that simultaneously asserts the national interest in quality schools and in equal access to education, with assistance for those with special needs.

To attain improvement in quality, we have proposed a number of new programs designed to strengthen teaching in curricular areas where national needs are especially great. To spur equal access to education, we recommend that current programs for special-needs students be supplemented by programs that will support school districts with large numbers of poor and immigrant pupils as well as districts that are experiencing fiscal difficulties. In addition, we have recommended that federal funding be provided to local school districts as an incentive to encourage new ways to help failing students.

In all of these programs, it must be kept in mind that equality of educational opportunity cannot be separated from educational quality. The nation is best served by offering our young people the most rigorous educational experience that we can. The federal government has a responsibility to help overcome the unevenness of state efforts. It will have to provide compensatory assistance, for some time to come, to those who are in need of special help, especially for students who must achieve English-language proficiency. But that does not mean abandoning a single standard of excellence. There cannot be a white standard or a black standard or a Hispanic standard when measuring educational performance.

The Task Force is aware that some of its proposals are costly. But we should be able to afford the price of a commitment to educational excellence. This nation's young people are our most precious and potentially our most productive asset, provided that we invest wisely in educating them. In our view, support for our program by Congress and the White House will demonstrate the value that they attach to better schooling for all.

Our proposed new approach for federal education policy will, we believe, stimulate a national reawakening of interest in educational excellence. But carrying out this policy requires our nation's political leaders to take an active part in supporting needed programs. It is no longer a cause that requires political courage. All across the country parents are demanding more of the schools, and in many cases the schools are already responding. We think the time is past due to offer a better education to all Americans. What it takes now is the political will to bring it about.

Background Paper
By Paul E. Peterson

ACKNOWLEDGMENTS

This paper has had the benefit of comments by members of the Task Force on Federal Elementary and Secondary Education Policy and a number of the staff members at the Twentieth Century Fund. In addition, I appreciate the advice and comments of Charles Bidwell, Fred Coombs, Michael Kirst, Henry Levin, and Hans Weiler. Portions of the paper were read and discussed before meetings of the American Educational Research Association, the National Academy of Education, the Committee on Public Policy Studies at the University of Chicago, and a small group of superintendents from the Chicago metropolitan area held at the Department of Education of the University of Chicago.

Research assistance was provided by Barry Rabe, Linda Wilson, and, especially, by Carol Peterson, who, among other things, proved to be an indefatigable sleuth who eliminated numerous errors from references, tables, and notes. Eve Dimon typed the initial draft, Annette Barrett assisted in the preparation of tables, and members of the Twentieth Century Fund staff assisted in the production of the final product. To all of these helpful assistants, I am grateful. Errors remain my responsibility alone.

1
IS THERE A CRISIS IN AMERICAN EDUCATION?

Americans have been proud of their public educational institutions, and rightly so. Our schools manifest the country's faith in every man's ability to comprehend public issues and to use his intelligence for society's betterment and its belief that the future is our collective responsibility. In the nineteenth century, when only limited educational opportunities, defined rigorously along class lines, were available in Europe, Americans created "common" schools that allowed all sectors of (at least white) society an opportunity to learn to read, write, and calculate. When secondary education in Europe was limited to classical training for a few, the American comprehensive high school provided both academic and vocational training to broad segments of the population. In 1920, for example, the estimated enrollment in U.S. secondary schools per 10,000 of population was 247, as compared with only 117 in Germany, 83 in England, and 61 in Sweden.[1]

Historically, public education has enjoyed broad social support. Business groups viewed schools as a training ground for workers, who would enter an increasingly sophisticated industrial empire that required higher levels of literacy and numeration. Trade unions found in compulsory education drives a useful handmaiden to their campaigns against child labor. Middle-class, reform-minded professionals, often themselves beneficiaries of a growing educational system, accepted John Stuart Mill's argument that knowledge and democracy were essential for one another.

The practice of schooling, however, was never as glorious as the statements of principles enunciated by such educators as Horace Mann and John Dewey. In the nineteenth century, for example, the benefits

27

of the American public high school were enjoyed almost exclusively by the middle class. During the depressions of the 1890s and 1930s, fiscal support for public education was drastically cut by local governments suffering from rapidly diminishing tax revenues. There were also problems resulting from ethnic and racial prejudices. For example, while many public schools taught Germans in their own language during the nineteenth century, this group found it virtually impossible to secure such instruction after World War I. Blacks and Orientals were excluded from public schools for generations in many parts of the United States; even after they were given formal access to schools, the education they received was poorly financed and offered in inferior settings. As the historical data in chapter 2 reveal, actual levels of public support for education in the past fell far short of current standards.[2]

Yet educational programs improved with each passing decade. Expenditures per pupil went up, pupil/teacher ratios declined, teachers' salaries increased, and the quality of the physical plant was upgraded. Schools began to provide a more diverse curriculum, extracurricular activities expanded, evening schools were established, kindergarten and preschool programs were founded, and school lunch programs became a stable part of the school day. After World War I, blacks were admitted to high schools in the South, and after World War II, steps were taken to equalize the distribution of educational resources across racial lines. As more was expected of the educational system, schools became more complex, diverse institutions.

Historically, American schools have been touchstones of the country's political health and economic prosperity. Thus, it is not surprising that, at a time when the nation's economic well-being is questioned and its political foundations seem to be less secure, many have raised doubts about American educational institutions. "There is not much time left," writes Carl L. Marburger of the National Committee for Citizens in Education, "for the public school system of this country to be dramatically reshaped, or it will not continue to exist as a viable and significant institution."[3] Cynthia Parsons, education editor of the *Christian Science Monitor*, urges, "We need to hear again, and from the highest levels of government, just why we offer free public schooling to all who live in our land. We need to know why a democracy and free public schooling are mutually reinforcing concepts."[4] And Albert Shanker, president of the American Federation of Teachers, states, "Today, public education in America is caught in a curious 'Catch-22' vise which threatens its very survival."[5]

Expressions of concern come from diverse quarters, and recommendations reflect the way the problems are perceived. Max Rafferty, a professor of education at Troy State University in Alabama, complains that education "has been used to promote such trivial goals as life adjustment, in-groupness and acceptance of the child by his peers instead of concentrating on subject matter and eventual learning tools."[6] Terry Herndon, the executive director of the National Education Association, views the problems as primarily fiscal:

> Our public schools are being asked to do more and more, even as experts proclaim that funding levels are not sufficient to meet prior expectations. Many local and state governments have exhausted their taxing capabilities and simply cannot provide comprehensive educational opportunity for all of their diverse students.[7]

Similarly, Michael W. Kirst, a professor of education at Stanford University, has asserted:

> The American public has chosen to use public schools as the national problem solver. . . . Local board members and school staffs are faced with insurmountable tasks such as alleviating racial and ethnic segregation, assimilating hundreds of . . . non-English speaking immigrants and refugees, and assuring equal educational opportunity for special needs students. Expected to handle these problems with relatively small resources, school people become extremely frustrated. Their resources and energies are drained away from academic programs. . . . [8]

And in the words of Albert H. Quie, former ranking minority member of the House Labor and Education Committee:

> Schools will need to address living in an interdependent world of limits, a slow-growth economy, labor scarcity, shifting age and population distribution, taxpayer resistance, increased public demands for educational accountability, demands for continuous lifelong education, continued involvement of the courts in ensuring equal access to education, innovations in technology, and competition from other services for public funds. Given these and other complex forces, it is crucial that we anticipate and plan for change, thereby helping our education system respond in deliberate, provocative ways.[9]

But expressions of concern and a sense of crisis are not new in American education. At the turn of the century, reformers uncovered high rates of so-called retardation in the public schools, that is, students two or more years older than the age considered appropriate for a particular grade; the schools responded by promoting students as much on the basis of age as on the basis of ability. In the 1920s, schools were said to be "inefficient"; educational experts undertook surveys in one major city after another, recommending such remedies as junior high schools and "platooning" (using school facilities more efficiently by moving children from class to class and onto the playground for supervised play when other children were using the available rooms). During the 1930s, local government fiscal crises left teachers unpaid and angry. In the 1950s, the Russian "Sputnik" generated widespread concern about the scientific training being offered in the public schools. In the 1960s, overbureaucratization, underinvolvement by parents, and racial segregation were considered the major problems.

The frequency with which crises have been identified in American education suggests that caution be exercised in characterizing educational difficulties, so that the rhetoric used does not automatically escalate problems into something more. As Harold Howe II, former commissioner of education, recently observed:

> When we overemphasize our problems, it is easy to forget our achievements. . . . For a country where each succeeding generation has for 100 years been more literate than the preceding one, we have an unbalanced view that places our educational problems, of which we have plenty, on center stage and shoves our achievements into the wings. There is not a country in the world with as complex a society and as tumultuous a history that can point to an education establishment as open, as diverse, and as excellent as ours.[10]

This admonition is worth serious reflection. Still, in the current discussion of educational problems, there is one issue that is not found in previous debates: the role of the federal government. It is possible to discount suggestions of crisis and still wonder whether the recent federal involvement in education has not had unintended, pernicious consequences. Indeed, the adverse effects of increasing federal regulation and control have now taken an equal place with the traditional and continuing areas of concern—fiscal difficulties, educational standards, and equal access to education—in analyses of educational problems.

Many familiar with American educational institutions believe the federal role to be excessive. Anne Campbell, commissioner of education for the state of Nebraska, insists that "prescriptive federal legislation and regulations are increasingly limiting the latitude within which states and local districts can work. In areas such as vocational education, education of the handicapped, and bilingual education, there is far too much specificity in federal directives."[11] David Savage, education editor for the *Los Angeles Times*, adds:

If Title I [the major compensatory education program] were the only aid program, there would be enough paperwork to keep everyone busy. But over the past 20 years, new education programs have sprouted up like fast food franchises along the highway. . . . The U.S. Office of Education used to count 134 different programs each with its own set of grant regulations, its own application, its own grant competition, and its own distribution network. The Education Department has no authority to eliminate a single one of these programs, to combine it with another, or to alter it in any way.[12]

And as J. Myron Atkin, dean of the Stanford School of Education, recently observed, "As power shifts from teacher to politician and civil servant, the new governmental assertiveness has effects in the classroom that are not always positive."[13] In Albert Shanker's words, "More and more decisions are being made by federal bureaucrats, state legislatures, financial control boards or budget officials at the federal and state levels. While control is slipping away from local officials, it is not being concentrated elsewhere. Power over the schools is being fragmented in a hundred different directions."[14] Joseph M. Cronin, while state superintendent of education for the state of Illinois, summarized the picture in these stark terms:

Most of the signals point to an increasingly centralized system and national education policy. This trend may, in fact, increase certain kinds of education opportunity while diminishing the traditional options of local and state governments. The junior partner [the federal government] is taking over the firm through sheer aggressiveness, while the senior partners fret about additional paperwork but graciously accept the extra income.[15]

These concerns about excessive federal interference in local school policy have been expressed in no uncertain terms by President Ronald Reagan. In his words, "Look at the record. Federal spending on education soared eightfold in the last 20 years, rising much faster than inflation. But during the same period, scholastic aptitude test scores went down, down and down."[16] The Reagan administration proposed in early 1981 that forty-four elementary- and secondary-education grant programs be consolidated into two block grants, one of which would be allocated among the states and the other among local school districts. According to the new administration, "These block grants will shift control over education policy away from the Federal Government and back to State and local authorities—where it constitutionally and historically belongs."[17]

These recommendations, considered on Capitol Hill during the hectic spring and summer of 1981, proved to be highly controversial. Beneficiaries of existing categorical programs sought to protect these programs from the budgetary ax; counterproposals were offered by House and Senate subcommittees; every week brought new rumors of major changes in program definition. Only lengthy deliberations within the conference committee could reconcile the bills emerging from each House. In the end, while significant budgetary cuts and a number of major policy innovations were made, the structure of federal education policy had been altered less than had once seemed likely.

Two of the major categorical programs—the Emergency School Aid program and the instructional resources program originally established by the National Defense Education Act—were folded together with a host of smaller programs into a block grant much as the Reagan administration had proposed. In addition, as can be seen in Table 3–1, funding levels were cut, so that the overall level of support for 1982 was roughly 25 percent below that of the previous fiscal year. However, four major categorical programs in education remained essentially intact, though at reduced funding levels: compensatory education, bilingual education, vocational education, and special education. Impact aid, though left as a separate program, suffered especially severe budgetary reductions.

Because the process by which these changes were introduced was hurried and hectic, the outcome represents a compromise among competing interests, not a consensus on the new direction federal education policy should take. The legislation was not considered in congressional hearings or given detailed scrutiny by the relevant congressional subcommittees. Deliberations on the floor of Congress focused on overall fiscal and economic policy, not on the particulars in education. Many groups in Congress remain committed to preserving and extending categorical programs. On the other hand, the Reagan administration publicly indicated that it would continue to seek further simplifications in federal regulations and guidelines—particularly in the area of special education.

As one administration official observed when the budget was being enacted, "What we've got [in the way of block grants] shows a significant start in reversing the direction of government. [Yet] the administration—and the President especially—has not indicated that it wants to back away from what was [initially] proposed. . . . The proposals are probably going to be considered in other vehicles in addition [to the 1981 budgetary process]."[18] Two months later, Terrel Bell, the new secretary of education, appointed a commission to study the quality of American education, and in 1983 a new program calling for increased emphasis on mathematics and science was proposed. In addition to these developments, the Reagan administration advocated tax credits for those parents who send their children to nonpublic schools. Clearly, even while some changes in the federal role in education are being made, many issues still remain active on the policy agenda.

In order to assess the future direction that federal education policy will take, three broad questions need to be asked: (1) What is the condition of American education? (2) What impact has federal policy had on that condition? (3) What, if anything, needs to be done?

In addressing the first question, chapter 2 illustrates how the continuous expansion of education in earlier decades slowed dramatically and may even have reversed itself as the 1970s came to a close. It documents how the decline in the number of children in the 1970s and 1980s reduced the demand for educational services, causing, among other things, a drop in teachers' salaries in real dollars. These declines were matched by a slide in public confidence in the schools, although this change in public opinion paralleled increasing public skepticism more generally. In the past ten years, along with a drop in enrollment and a decline in public confidence, public schools have had to accept a leveling off of the steep fiscal growth that they enjoyed in the 1960s and early 1970s. In addition, they have lost students to nonpublic schools (although non-public-school attendance still falls short of its postwar high). Student performance also has been uneven. While children at the primary level do seem to learn more, especially in reading, than did their counterparts a few years earlier, secondary students are doing less well, especially in science and mathematics. Scholastic aptitude test scores also have fallen, and the number of white students dropping out of school has increased.

To what extent are these trends influenced by federal policy? The answer to this—given in chapters 3, 4, and 5—is, probably, not much. Federal financing of public schools never exceeded 10 percent of the total cost. The traditional federal role has called for minimal national direction and guidance, and, even with the redefinition of national policy that occurred around 1965, when equal opportunity came to center stage, federal influence has been exercised only in circumscribed areas such as compensatory education, school desegregation, bilingual education, and programs for the handicapped. As chapters 4 and 5 demonstrate, these programs introduced considerably more federal direction and guidance. The results of such federal initiatives were frequently mixed. While on the positive side the public became more aware of equal education opportunity issues, the federal guidelines encumbered local decisionmaking with unnecessary restrictions and misconceived directives. Taken as a whole, the increased federal role has had only modest effects on our educational system.

This does not imply that changes need not be made. It merely means that policymakers must appreciate the limits of the federal role. Chapter 6 includes a consideration of future directions for federal elementary- and secondary-education policy. Here, there is a need for balance, both with respect to the emphasis on quality and equality as well as with respect to the question of federal direction and local autonomy. The almost exclusive federal emphasis on equality of educational opportunity, which has characterized federal policy in the recent past, is sometimes taken to imply that the quality of the schools is unimportant to the nation as a whole. To avoid leaving such an impression, both the ideals of quality and equality need to be continuously addressed to keep federal policy in equilibrium. Even though the federal government cannot directly upgrade the quality of American classrooms, it must complement its current equal opportunity programs with a number of steps, both symbolic and substantive, to emphasize its simultaneous commitment to educational quality. The federal government also must address itself to administrative issues. Since education is an art, not a science, its processes are not subject to precise delineation by omniscient central administrators. Although federal purposes must be clear, the exercise of local judgment also is essential.

In sum, this background paper assesses the current state of American education, describes and evaluates the impact of federal policy on education, and provides a framework for evaluating recommendations for change. Many issues in this short book cannot be treated with the comprehensiveness they deserve. Certain important areas of federal policy must be put aside altogether. The book does not, for example, explore the numerous ways in which the federal government has altered the structure of higher education in the United States. Nor does it analyze the way in which federally funded manpower training and youth employment programs fit in—or fail to fit in—with the mainstream of secondary education. It does not even consider the many subtle ways in which the federal government, by sponsoring conferences, commissions, research laboratories, and major research undertakings, has indirectly influenced trends in elementary and secondary education.

The pages that follow will focus on the most financially costly and politically salient problem now confronting federal policymakers: how should the federal government directly assist in the maintenance and operation of the nation's elementary and secondary schools. The distance American schools have traveled in the postwar period, the way in which the federal role has evolved, and some of the issues and problems that have accompanied an expanding, although still limited, federal role are examined. The analysis of these questions is neither an apology for the status quo nor an alarmist call for dramatic change. Overall, many trends in American education seem to be more positive than negative. While areas of deficiency can be discerned, there is little evidence for concluding that the American system of education is in serious trouble, much less that it has failed.

It becomes clear that the consequences of federal policy for American education are less dramatic than implied in much public commentary. It is true that many federal regulations seem excessively burdensome, require otherwise unnecessary administrative activity, and interfere with local flexibility in resource allocation. It is especially unfortunate that federal guidelines have encouraged a form of compensatory education that "pulls" the disadvantaged child "out" of his or her daily classroom for special attention. Also, federal regulations have required higher levels of services to the handicapped without providing local educational authorities with commensurate fiscal resources. These and other policies have left school districts with difficulties and problems that could be eased by changes in federal regulatory controls.

But just because federal guidelines are in need of modification does not mean that the federal role in education should be eliminated altogether. Even though federal fiscal involvement has always been supplemental to state and local efforts, it serves the important function of highlighting the national interest in equal access to quality education. Because the economic and fiscal constraints on state and local governments make it especially difficult to provide education for the disadvantaged, federal contributions to equal opportunity have been particularly significant. Prior to federal involvement, programming for those who spoke little English, for the handicapped, and for low-income groups in general was insufficient. Just as welfare policy has become a national responsibility, so educational programs for the disadvantaged need active federal support. The federal role in education should also be to stimulate efforts to enhance the quality of the nation's public schools. Here, federal policy cannot regulate as it did in the equal opportunity area, but federal initiative can clarify national goals in ways not open to any other level of government or to any private concern.

2
TRENDS IN AMERICAN EDUCATION: FROM RAPID GROWTH TO UNEASY STABILITY

Federal policy is but one of many influences on the shape and direction of American education. While it is praised by some as essential for preserving equality of opportunity and condemned by others for placing public schools into an administrative straitjacket, its actual impact is probably far more modest than either apologists or critics suggest. As shown in Table 2–1, in 1979–80 the federal government's fiscal contribution covered only 9.8 percent of the current expenditures of the country's elementary and secondary public schools. While this was more than double the percentage contribution made two decades ago, and thus represents a substantial increase in the federal role, the figures also demonstrate that much that happens in American schools is the product of decisions made at state and local levels. Indeed, as Table 2–1 also shows, the shift over the past two decades from local to state financing of education is as substantial a fiscal development as the increased federal role.

A proper assessment of the federal role in education, therefore, must place federal policy developments in a larger context and then determine to what extent the federal role is responsible for the trends in education. In this regard, it is frequently asserted that three significant trends may be traced in American education: first, that school enrollments have declined as the baby-boom generation was followed by the baby-bust generation; second, that public confidence in and fiscal support for education have eroded badly in recent years; third, that the quality of educational instruction and the level of pupil performance have deteriorated significantly. For some, federal policy is responsible

Table 2-1 Sources of Public-School Revenue Receipts and the Percentage Spent on Public
           Elementary- and Secondary-School Current Expenditures

	1929-30	1939-40	1949-50	1959-60	1969-70	1979-80
Total revenue receipts (in billions)	$2.09	$2.26	$5.44	$14.75	$40.27	$96.9
Percent of revenue from:						
Federal government	.4%	1.8%	2.9%	4.4%	8.0%	9.8%
State governments	16.9	30.3	39.8	39.1	39.9	46.8
Local sources	82.7	68.0	57.3	56.5	52.1	43.4
Total %	100.0%	100.1%	100.0%	100.0%	100.0%	100.0%
Total expenditures for all public schools (in billions)	$2.32	$2.34	$5.84	$15.61	$40.68	$96.0
Percent of total expenditures for elementary and secondary school current expenditures	79.6%	82.8%	80.3%	70.0%	84.1%	90.6%

Source: Department of Education, National Center for Education Statistics, *Digest of Education Statistics*
         (Washington, D.C.: Government Printing Office, 1980, 1981, 1982 eds.).

for the overall sense of decline that these separate trends represent. For others, federal policy is the hope for arresting these changes. But before these issues can be addressed, we must first assess the present trajectory of our educational institutions. Thus, in this chapter I shall explore the available evidence on changes occurring in American education.

The data speak for themselves. Significantly, they provide little support for the sense of decline and deterioration in education that many believe currently exists. To be sure, declining pupil enrollments provide fewer opportunities for those employed in the educational system, and teachers' salaries are not as handsome as they were in the early 1970s. But if the problem of central concern is the learning environment available to students, not the employment prospects available to adults, then the evidence of decline is very recent and much more limited than the claims of crisis imply. While the quality of schools varies enormously from one part of the country to another, and from one neighborhood to another in any single city, signs of nationwide decay are difficult to ascertain. To the extent that such signs exist, the evidence does point to the secondary school as meriting special concern; however, it is the secondary school that has been least touched by federal policy.

I present these overall conclusions now, so that the reader can check them against the data in the following pages. I shall begin with the undeniable demographic changes, then turn to questions of financing and staffing in education, then explore public opinion about schools, and finally examine the evidence on the results of schooling.

Demographic Changes

The number of school-age children has declined steadily since 1970 and, at the secondary-school level, will continue to do so for another decade. As shown in Table 2-2, the drop is particularly high among

Table 2-2 Elementary- and Secondary–School-Age Population of the United States, by Race and with Projections, 1965–90

| | (numbers in millions) | | | | % |
	White	Black	Other	Total	Minority
5 to 13 years[a]					
1965	30.6	4.7	.4	35.7	14.3
1970	31.1	5.0	.5	36.6	15.0
1975	28.0	4.8	.6	33.4	16.2
1980	24.9	4.6	.7	30.2	17.5
1985[b]	23.8	4.5	.9	29.2	18.5
1990[b]	26.8	4.7	1.0	32.5	17.5
14 to 17 years[a]					
1965	12.3	1.7	.2	14.2	13.4
1970	13.6	2.1	.3	16.0	15.0
1975	14.3	2.3	.4	17.0	15.9
1980	13.1	2.3	.4	15.8	17.1
1985[b]	11.8	2.2	.4	14.4	18.1
1990[b]	10.3	2.1	.4	12.8	19.5
Percentage Change					
5 to 13 years					
1965–70	1.6	6.4	20.2[c]	2.5	
1970–75	−10.0	−3.9	19.4[c]	−8.7	
1975–80	−11.2	−4.9	23.8[c]	−9.7	
1980–85	−4.5	−2.8	20.0[c]	−3.6	
1985–90	12.8	6.2	17.7[c]	11.9	
14 to 17 years					
1965–70	11.0	20.8	33.6[c]	12.4	
1970–75	5.2	11.9	32.0[c]	6.4	
1975–80	−8.4	−.7	19.0[c]	−6.9	
1980–85	−9.9	−5.2	16.9[c]	−8.7	
1985–90	−13.1	−6.6	19.0[c]	−11.3	

Source: Department of Education, National Center for Education Statistics, *The Condition of Education* (Washington, D.C.: Government Printing Office, 1980).
a. Estimates as of July 1 of each year. Includes Armed Forces overseas.
b. Census Series II projections.
c. Based on unrounded numbers.

white students, where, at the elementary-school level, there was a 10 percent decline from 1970 to 1975 and an 11 percent drop from 1975 to 1980. The rate of decline is now slowing and is expected to reverse itself in the late 1980s. The percentage decline in the number of black school-age children is somewhat less than the percentage decrease among whites, and the percentage of Americans from other racial backgrounds has been sharply increasing (although, obviously, from a small base). The net effect of these changes is a continuing rise in the percentage of young Americans who are members of a racial minority. Whereas they comprised 15 percent of the secondary-school-age population in 1970, they are expected to form 19.5 percent of that population in 1990.

What is occurring in the population at large is reflected in exaggerated form in public-school enrollments. As shown in Table 2-3, the enrollment declines that first hit the public elementary schools in the 1970s are now being felt at the secondary-school level. At the same time that enrollment is falling, the composition of the public school is changing (see Table 2-4). Because white pupils are more likely than minority pupils to attend private or parochial schools, the percentage of minority pupils in the public schools increased from 17.7 percent in 1970 to 24.1 percent in 1980.

National trends obscure a great deal of regional variation. As shown

Table 2-3 Public Elementary- and Secondary–School Enrollment, Fall 1968 to Fall 1990

	Grade Level		
Fall of Year	K–12 Total	K–8	9–12
	(in millions)		
1968	44.9	32.2	12.7
1971	46.1	32.3	13.8
1974	45.1	30.9	14.1
1977	43.6	29.3	14.2
1980[a]	41.0	27.7	13.3
1983[b]	39.2	27.0	12.1
1986[b]	39.5	27.4	12.1
1990[b]	41.3	30.2	11.0

Sources: Department of Education, National Center for Education Statistics, *Projections of Education Statistics to 1988–89* (Washington, D.C.: Government Printing Office, 1981), and *Projections of Education Statistics to 1990–91* (Washington, D.C.: Government Printing Office, 1982).
a. Estimated.
b. Projected.

in Table 2-5, declining enrollments are aggravated in the Northeast and North Central regions by an overall shift in the population to the South and West, a process that is expected to be as pronounced in the 1980s as it was in the 1970s.

Teacher Employment and Salaries

Changes in the demographic structure of the American population have had a direct effect on the prospects for employment in the field of education. At the very time that falling enrollments have lowered the de-

Table 2-4 Elementary- and Secondary–Public-School Enrollment, By Race, 1970–80

| | Percent Racial Composition | | | | |
	White	Black	Hispanic	Total %	Total (in millions)
1970	82.2	13.2	4.5	99.9	51,309
1972	81.5	13.6	4.9	100.0	50,744
1974	81.3	13.5	5.2	100.0	50,053
1976	80.4	13.8	5.8	100.0	49,316
1980	76.0[a]	16.1	8.0	100.1	39,832

Sources: Department of Education, National Center for Education Statistics, *The Condition of Education* (Washington, D.C.: Government Printing Office, 1979), and *Digest of Education Statistics* (Washington, D.C.: Government Printing Office, 1980); Department of Health, Education, and Welfare, Office for Civil Rights, *Distribution of Students by Racial/Ethnic Composition of Schools,* 1970–76 (Washington, D.C.: Government Printing Office, August 1978).
a. Includes 1.9 percent Asian and 0.8 percent American Indian/Alaskan native.

Table 2-5 Population Changes in the United States, by Region and with Projections, 1970–90

| | | Percent Change[a] | | | |
Region	Census April 1970 (in millions)	1970 to 1975	1975 to 1980	1980 to 1985	1985 to 1990
United States	203.3	4.8	4.0	4.8	4.6
Northeast	49.1	.8	.8	1.9	2.0
North Central	56.6	1.8	1.4	2.5	2.5
South	62.8	8.3	7.1	7.4	6.7
West	34.8	8.8	7.0	7.3	6.5

Source: Department of Education, National Center for Education Statistics, *The Condition of Education* (Washington, D.C.: Government Printing Office, 1980).
a. Details may not add to totals because of rounding. Projected data from Census Series II-B.

mand for teachers, the number of people qualified to teach has grown. As shown in Table 2-6, for nearly a decade there has been an oversupply of qualified personnel, and, while there may be some shortages in certain fields, this trend is likely to continue until the mid-1980s.

There are several reasons for the abundant supply of teachers. First, the baby-boom generation entered the labor market in the 1970s, increasing the number of young adults seeking employment. Second, the percentage of the population that earned a college degree, and was thereby able to qualify for teaching positions, increased substantially between 1960 and 1975. At the beginning of that period, only 11.0 percent of the 25–34 age group had completed sixteen or more years of education; by 1975, 21.4 percent had done so. Finally, other occupational opportunities for women, who traditionally have comprised the majority of elementary- and secondary-school teachers and who still constituted 66.2 percent of the teaching force in 1979 (as compared with 72.2 percent in 1960), did not open up dramatically. Because the earnings of fulltime, four-year-college-educated females continued to be only 59 percent of those of their male counterparts, teaching as a career has remained financially attractive to women seeking employment. Also, the supply of available teachers remained at a high level as a consequence of the fact that the percentage of unmarried women and the percentage of married women willing to reenter the labor market after childbirth remained relatively constant during the 1970s.[1]

In the 1980s, employment prospects for those entering the field of education may improve somewhat: the size of the population entering

Table 2-6 Estimated Supply of New Teachers Compared with Estimated Total Demand for Additional Teachers in Regular Public Elementary and Secondary Schools, 1969–88

Year	Estimated Supply of New Teachers	Estimated Total Demand for Additional Teachers	Supply of New Teachers as a Percent of Total Demand for Additional Teachers
	in thousands		
1969–73	1,492	990	150.7
1974–78	1,132	819	138.2
1979–83	893	622	143.6
1984–88	780	861	90.6

Sources: Department of Education, National Center for Education Statistics, *The Condition of Education* (Washington, D.C.: Government Printing Office, 1980); National Education Association, *Teacher Supply and Demand in Public Schools* (Washington, D.C.: National Education Association of the United States, 1973, 1977, 1978 eds.); and Department of Education, National Center for Education Statistics, *Projection of Education Statistics to 1988–89* (Washington, D.C.: Government Printing Office, 1980).

the labor market will decrease; alternative occupational opportunities for women may be greater; the demand for new teachers will increase at the elementary-school level, where female teachers are disproportionately concentrated; and a steep rise in the percentage of the population with a college degree is not likely. But current prospects for employment in the education system are less than buoyant. Table 2–7 shows that in 1981, in adjusted dollars, the average annual salary of the public-school instructional staff had declined by 13.4 percent since salaries peaked in 1976, and by 12.2 percent since 1970. In 1976, teacher salaries had reached a historic high. At that time, the nation's schools were bulging with baby-boom children, and the number of college graduates with degrees in education could not keep up with the demand for teachers. But while the halcyon days of the 1970s could not continue in a period marked by a decline in the demand for teachers, a 12 percent real decline in teachers' earning power certainly contributes to current discontent in education. At the same time, salary declines have not induced a major exodus from the nation's schools. On the contrary, the diminished number of entrants into teaching has meant an increase in the number of years the average teacher has held his position. (See Table 2–8.)

Table 2–7   Average Annual Salary of Instructional Staff in Public Elementary and Secondary Schools, 1929–30 to 1980–81

School Year	Salary per Member of Instructional Staff (unadjusted dollars)	Salary per Member of Instructional Staff (adjusted dollars, 1978–79 purchasing power)[a]
1929–30	$ 1,420	$ 5,547
1939–40	1,441	7,063
1949–50	3,010	8,708
1959–60	5,174	11,547
1969–70	8,840	16,035
1975–76	13,155[b]	16,248[b]
1978–79	15,615[b]	15,615[b]
1980–81	18,409[b]	14,075[b]

Sources: Department of Education, National Center for Education Statistics, *Digest of Education Statistics* (Washington, D.C.: Government Printing Office, 1980), and *Statistics of State School Systems* (Washington, D.C.: Government Printing Office, various years); and National Education Association, *Estimates of School Statistics* (Washington, D.C.: National Education Association of the United States, 1978–79).

a. Based on the consumer price index, prepared by the Bureau of Labor Statistics, Department of Labor.

b. Based on estimates.

Table 2–8   Median Years on Current Job of Professional, Technical, and
            Kindred Workers, by Sex and Occupation, January 1973 and
            January 1978

Sex and Occupation	1973	1978
Male		
Professional, technical workers	4.8	4.8
Teachers (except college)	4.4	6.5
Physicians, dentists and related practitioners	7.0	5.5
Engineers	6.0	6.0
Engineering and science technicians	5.0	3.7
Other professionals	4.5	3.7
Female		
Professional, technical workers	3.4	3.6
Teachers (except college)	3.7	4.7
Physicians, dentists, and related practitioners	3.1	3.5
Engineers	a	a
Engineering and science technicians	2.6	2.7
Other professionals	3.2	2.7

Sources: Department of Education, National Center for Education Statistics, *The Condition of
          Education* (Washington, D.C.: Government Printing Office, 1980); Department of
          Labor, Bureau of Labor Statistics, unpublished tabulations.
          a. Base less than 75,000.

Education Expenditures

As unsatisfactory as teacher salaries now seem to be, the salary and
employment prospects of teachers should not be confused with the
well-being of pupils in the nation's schools. When viewed from the
perspective of the pupil, the resources available for education might be
a better yardstick. The point of comparison chosen will determine
whether or not there has been a decline in these resources. When 1960
expenditures are compared with those of 1981, one finds a dramatic
increase, from $15.6 billion to $99.8 billion. (See Table 2-9.) While
much of this increase is due to inflationary pressures, even in constant
dollars annual expenditures over the two decades increased by more
than $40 billion. Moreover, these increases occurred when the need for
capital outlays was declining. After the rapid expansion of plant facilities during the late 1940s and the 1950s, and in response to pressures
to accommodate the baby-boom generation, schools nationwide
enjoyed excess plant capacity and had minimal construction needs. As
a result, the percentage of educational expenditures for capital pur-

Table 2-9 Public Elementary- and Secondary-School Expenditures, 1929-30 to 1980-81

	1929-30	1939-40	1949-50	1959-60	1969-70	1977-78	1979-80	1980-81
				(billions of dollars)				
Total expenditures								
Current $	$2.3	$2.3	$5.8	$15.6	$40.7	$80.8	$96.0	$99.8
Constant $[a]	9.8	12.0	17.6	38.5	78.3	93.2	87.7	80.4
Percent devoted to elementary and secondary schools								
Current expenditures	79.6%	82.8%	80.3%	79.0%	84.1%	90.5%	90.6%	90.1%
Capital outlay	16.0	11.0	17.4	17.0	11.5	6.4	6.8	6.7
Interest on debt	4.0	5.6	1.7	3.1	2.9	2.3	2.0	1.9
Other programs[b]	.4	.6	.6	.8	1.6	.7	.6	1.3
Total percent	100.0%	100.0%	100.0%	99.9%	100.1%	99.9%	100.0%	100.0%

Source: Department of Education, National Center for Education Statistics, *Digest of Education Statistics* (Washington, D.C.: Government Printing Office, 1980, 1982 eds.).
a. 1979 = 100
b. Other programs include attendance, health, transportation and food services, and pupil activities paid for out of tax revenues. Prior to 1959-60, it also includes community services.

poses declined from 17 percent in 1959-60 to 6.7 percent in 1980-81, and current, noncapital expenditures now account for 90 percent of total expenditures. When comparisons are made between 1978 and 1981, the picture is less satisfying. While expenditures in current dollars continued to increase, in adjusted dollars they declined by 12.8 percent. Much of this decrease can be explained by the 6.7 percent decline in the number of children attending public schools between 1977 and 1980 and the 9.8 percent drop in teacher salaries between 1978 and 1981. But even when viewed optimistically, clearly public fiscal support for education reached its peak in the late 1970s.

Examination of school expenditures on a per pupil basis also reveals that the period of sustained growth came to an end in the late 1970s. In every decade since 1940, there has been a steep increment (in adjusted dollars) in the level of per pupil expenditures (see Table 2-10). From 1960 to 1970, expenditures in noninflated dollars increased from $926 to $1,569 per pupil, and in the most recent decade, they increased again to $2,396. Between 1978 and 1980, however, there was very little increase in per pupil expenditures. While as of 1980 there was no apparent decline, once again it seems that a peak had been attained.

Still a third indicator reveals a leveling off of fiscal support after a long period of growth. The percentage of the gross national product (GNP) allocated for current public-school expenditures increased steeply throughout the postwar period. As shown in Table 2-11, the United States spent only 1.8 percent of its resources on education in 1949, but by 1979, 4 percent was allocated for education. Between 1979 and 1981, educational expenditure as a percentage of GNP fell to 3.3

MAKING THE GRADE

Table 2–10 Current Expenditure per Pupil in Average Daily Attendance in Public Elementary and Secondary Schools, the United States, 1929–30 to 1979–80

School Year	Unadjusted Dollars	Adjusted Dollars (1979 purchasing power)[a]
1929–30	$ 87	$ 373
1939–40	88	458
1949–50	209	633
1959–60	375	926
1969–70	816	1,569
1977–78	2,002	2,315
1979–80	2,275	2,396

Source: Department of Education, National Center for Education Statistics, *Digest of Education Statistics* (Washington, D.C.: Government Printing Office, 1980, 1982 eds.).
a. Based on the consumer price index, prepared by the Bureau of Labor Statistics, Department of Labor.

Table 2–11 Gross National Product (GNP) Related to Current Expenditures for Public Elementary and Secondary Education, Health, and Defense, 1949–81

Calendar Year	GNP	Current Expenditures for Education		Expenditures for health		Expenditures for defense	
		Total	% of GNP	Total	% of GNP	Total	% of GNP
		(in billions–unadjusted dollars)					
1949	$ 258.0	$ 4.7	1.8%	$ 11.6	4.5%	$ 13.2	5.1%
1959	486.5	12.3	2.5	24.9	5.1	45.6	9.4
1969	935.5	34.2	3.7	64.8	6.9	76.3	8.2
1975	1,528.8	62.1	4.1	131.5	8.6	83.7	5.5
1979	2,395.4	95.4	4.0	192.4[a]	9.1[a]	99.5[a]	4.7[a]
1981	2,925.5[b]	97.5[c]	3.3	247.2[b]	9.4	188.8[c]	6.5

Sources: Department of Commerce, Bureau of the Census: *Statistical Abstract of the United States* (Washington, D.C.: Government Printing Office, 1981); Department of Education, National Center for Education Statistics, *The Condition of Education* (Washington, D.C.: Government Printing Office, 1980).
a. These figures are for 1978, based on the 1978 GNP of $2,106.6.
b. These figures are for 1980, based on the 1980 GNP of $2,626.1.
c. Estimated.

percent. While some of that drop was due to the decreased number of public-school pupils and to a new balance in the demand and supply of teachers, it also reflects the fact that the public commitment to education had not continued to spiral upward.

What these expenditure patterns reveal is quite consistent with other indicators of resource allocation to education. Figure 2–1 shows a

Figure 2–1 Classroom Teachers and Student–Teacher Ratios in Elementary/Secondary Schools

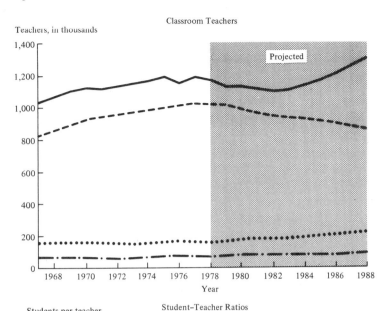

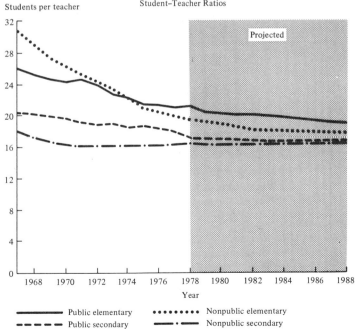

Source: Department of Education, National Center for Education Statistics, *The Condition of Education* (Washington, D.C.: Government Printing Office, 1980).

marked decline in the pupil-teacher ratio between 1968 and 1978, but it also projects a flattening of this curve in the 1980s. And while recent information on the professional preparation of teachers is not yet available, between 1961 and 1976, the percent that had earned a master's degree increased from 23.5 to 37.2.[2]

These national trends again obscure considerable regional variation. Population movements and changes in the location of business and industrial activity have left many cities of the Northeast and Midwest with fewer resources for educational purposes. The Chicago school system, for example, did not pay teachers' salaries for several weeks in the fall of 1979, because it was unable to raise the necessary revenues. While some of the school board's difficulties stemmed from poor management, the changing economic condition of the city aggravated the school system's problems. Under these pressures, per pupil expenditures, after climbing steadily for decades, increased only slightly (in constant dollars) between 1970 and 1981. On the other hand, the pupil to teacher ratio in the city fell from 20.8 in 1970 to 16.5 in 1981. (See Table 2-12.) Even under one of the most difficult situations, it seems the public schools did not fare badly. In large cities more generally, per pupil expenditures and teachers' salaries in 1979-80 were higher than in the United States as a whole, and pupil to teacher ratios were only slightly larger (see Table 2-13).

Public Support for Education

While these data show that resource allocation for education recently reached a plateau after decades of growth, many in education believe that public support is rapidly eroding and that a period of sustained decline has already set in. Information on public attitudes and on nonpublic-school attendance is frequently cited as evidence that Americans no longer have the same interest in the public schools that they once had. First, it is said that confidence in the public schools has steadily declined among the public at large. Gallup poll results, as shown in Table 2-14, indicate that the percentage of the population rating schools as deserving a grade of "A" or "B" slipped from a high of 48 percent in 1974 to 36 percent in 1981. At the same time, those giving the schools a low rating of "D" or "F" increased from 11 to 20 percent. While these findings are a matter of concern, the schools do continue to receive as much or more support than any other public institution, and the declines in public confidence experienced by the schools are less than that suffered by such a venerable institution as Congress (see Table 2-15). In any case, polling information only pro-

Table 2-12 Average Daily Attendance and per Pupil Expenditure, Chicago Public Schools, 1931–81

| | Number of teachers | Average daily attendance (ADA) | ADA per teacher | Per pupil expenditure in current and constant[a] dollars | | | | | |
| | | | | Elementary | | High School | | Total | |
				Current	Constant	Current	Constant	Current	Constant
1931	13,115	433,231	33.0	N.A.		N.A.		166	791
1940	13,796	404,808	29.3	N.A.		N.A.		143	740
1950	12,916	331,029	25.6	N.A.		N.A.		281	847
1960	16,529	427,894	25.9	435	1,066	608	1,490	510	1,250
1965	20,768	491,786	23.7	494	1,136	668	1,537	618	1,422
1970	24,194	502,778	20.8	845	1,580	1,246	2,329	1,186	2,217
1979[b]	25,514	411,234	16.1	1,940	1,940	2,300	2,300	2,045	2,045
1981[b]	24,958	411,144	16.5	2,656	2,139	3,310	2,665	2,836	2,273

Source: Monthly Reports of School Statistics, *Proceedings*, Board of Education, City of Chicago, for the relevant years; data on per pupil expenditure computed from Annual Financial Reports, in *Proceedings*.
a. Constant dollars are computed using 1979 = 100.
b. Figures for 1979 and 1981 were obtained from the staff of the Board of Education, and strict comparability with previous years cannot be assured.
N.A. = not available.

Table 2-13 Selected Statistics on Public Elementary and Secondary Schools in the United States as a Whole and in Twenty Large Cities, 1979–80

| | | | Average annual salary | |
	Pupils per teacher	Current expenditure per pupil in average daily attendance	Classroom teachers	Other professional educational staff[a]
United States as a whole	19.1	$2,095	$16,170	$17,375
Twenty large cities[b]	20.7	$2,691[c]	$19,523	$21,963[c]

Source: Department of Education, National Center for Education Statistics, *Digest of Education Statistics* (Washington, D.C.: Government Printing Office, 1982).
a. Includes salaries of curriculum specialists, library-media specialists, and guidance and counseling personnel only.
b. The twenty cities are Baltimore, Md.; Boston, Mass.; Chicago, Ill.; Cleveland, Ohio; Dallas, Texas; Detroit, Mich.; Houston, Texas; Indianapolis, Ind.; Los Angeles, Calif.; Memphis, Tenn.; Milwaukee, Wis.; New Orleans, La.; New York City; Philadelphia, Penn.; Phoenix, Ariz.; St. Louis, Mo.; San Antonio, Texas; San Diego, Calif.; San Francisco, Calif.; Washington, D.C.
c. Estimated, based on intermediate alternative projections from the National Center for Education Statistics.

vides the opinions of individuals as expressed to interviewers. These opinions may or may not reliably predict what people will actually do about educational matters if called upon to act.

In this regard, some have pointed with particular distress to signs of declining voter support for school bond referenda. Table 2–16 shows that both the number of bond referenda held and the percentage of referenda approved by the voters dropped sharply between 1964 and 1974, leading many to suggest that an aging, increasingly childless pop-

Table 2–14 Public Ratings of School Performance

Grade	1974	1975	1976	1977	1978	1979	1980	1981
	(percent of those polled)							
A	18	13	13	11	9	8	10	9
B	30	30	29	26	27	26	25	27
C	21	28	28	28	30	30	29	34
D	6	9	10	10	11	11	12	13
F	5	7	6	6	8	7	6	7

Source: Gallup Poll results as cited in *Phi Delta Kappan* (September 1980 and 1981).

Table 2–15 Percentage of Polled Population Expressing Confidence in Public Institutions

Institutions in Question[a]	1973	1975	1977	1979	1980
Public schools	58	N.A.	54	53	51
The military	N.A.	58	57	54	52
U.S. Supreme Court	44	49	46	45	47
Congress	42	40	40	34	34

Source: Gallup Poll from *San Jose Mercury*, November 6, 1980, as cited in Michael W. Kirst, "Loss of Support for Public Schools: Some Causes and Solutions," reprinted by permission of *Daedalus, Journal of the American Academy of Arts and Sciences* 110 (Summer 1981), p. 49.
a. The question asked by Gallup was the following: "I am going to read you a list of institutions in American society. Would you tell me how much confidence you, yourself, have in each one—a great deal, quite a lot, some, or very little?"
N.A. = not available.

ulation is no longer willing to provide educational services to those still in need of them. Although these claims cannot be discounted, it is far from clear that people interpret their self-interests so narrowly that they are unwilling to support public education unless their own children are attending school. Presumably, people are also concerned about the education of their nephews, nieces, and grandchildren, if not simply about the well-being of society as a whole.

Declining numbers of bond referenda may have been a function of the contraction in the school-age population, making fewer capital expansions and improvements necessary. In the late 1970s, the level of expenditures necessary for capital expansion could not be expected to match the level required at the height of the baby boom. As for the decline in voter support for bond proposals offered by school boards, it is possible that boards are making a less compelling case or that voters are becoming more concerned about increases in the property tax. As was shown in Table 2–1, there has been a gradual shift in the source of

Table 2-16 Results of Public-School Bond Elections: United States, 1961-62 to 1982

Fiscal year	Number of elections	Percent approved
1961-62	1,432	72.2
1962-63	2,048	72.4
1963-64	2,071	72.5
1964-65	2,041	74.7
1965-66	1,745	72.5
1966-67	1,625	66.6
1967-68	1,750	67.6
1968-69	1,341	56.8
1969-70	1,216	53.2
1970-71	1,086	46.7
1971-72	1,153	47.0
1972-73	1,273	56.5
1973-74	1,386	56.2
1974-75	929	46.3
1975-76	770	50.8
1976-77	858	55.6
1978	N.A.	61.0[a]
1979	N.A.	45.0[a]
1980	N.A.	55.0[a]
1981	N.A.	59.0[a]
1982	N.A.	73.0[a]

Sources: Department of Education, National Center for Education Statistics, *Digest of Education Statistics* (Washington, D.C.: Government Printing Office, 1980), and Annual Reports on Bond Sales for Public School Purposes; for 1978-82, *New York Times*, April 11, 1983, p. 9.
a. Estimates accurate to within 2 percent.
N.A. = not available.

fiscal support for education from local revenues, which are heavily dependent on the property tax, to state and national revenues, which rely on more elastic income and sales taxes. Declining support for bond referenda may have been a part of this larger trend; certainly it would be incorrect to conclude that in the 1970s, government leaders, or the voters who elected them, became unwilling to provide the necessary fiscal resources for education. Indeed, the most recent data show a dramatic upswing in bond referenda support. Approval rates returned to their 1962 high in 1982, climbing steadily upward after bottoming out in 1979.

A more serious sign of declining support for public schools is the move, by a significant number of parents, away from the public sector. The increasing willingness of parents to pay for private education, while still bearing the tax burden needed to support the public schools, may indicate deteriorating public-school services. Many commentators have noted with concern the expansion of non-public-school enrollments in communities undergoing school desegregation, and scholars have observed that in recent years Christian schools have more than doubled their enrollments.[3] Are Americans voting with their feet against public education?

Once again, the answer depends on the years for which non-public-school attendance rates are examined. As shown in Table 2–17, the percentage of pupils in nonpublic schools increased steadily from 1930 until it reached a high of 13.5 percent in 1960. After reaching that peak, non-public-school attendance fell to 9.8 percent in 1974; in the past few years, the percentage of pupils enrolled in nonpublic schools increased again to 12.4 percent, just short of its 1960 high. Many attribute recent increases in non-public-school attendance to a deterioration in the quality of public schools. Others believe that, as public schools have desegregated, nonpublic schools have capitalized on racist sentiments. Quite another explanation is the steady increase in the education and income levels of American families, especially those in which both husband and wife work. These families may have both a greater interest in and more resources for private education. Nonetheless, the increasing use of nonpublic schools, though hardly of epidemic propor-

Table 2–17 Private–School Enrollment as a Percentage of Total School Enrollment, 1930–81

	School Level			
	Kindergarten	Elementary School[a]	High School[b]	All levels
1930	6.9%	9.8%	7.1%	9.3%
1940	8.7	10.2	6.4	9.2
1950	11.3	12.2	10.4	11.8
1960	15.4	14.2	10.8	13.5
1968	17.1	12.5	9.6	12.0
1970	16.8	11.6	8.0	10.9
1972	15.9	11.0	7.6	10.3
1974	16.2	10.2	7.6	9.8
1976	15.1	10.3	7.6	9.9
1978	16.6	11.4	8.0	10.6
1981	└───── 13.3[c] ─────┘		10.4	12.4

Sources: Department of Education, National Center for Education Statistics, *Digest of Education Statistics* (Washington, D.C.: Government Printing Office, 1980, 1982 eds.); Department of Commerce, Bureau of the Census, *School Enrollment—Social Economic Characteristics of Students* (Washington, D.C.: Government Printing Office, October 1978).
  a. Grades 1–8.
  b. Grades 9–12.
  c. This figure represents a combined percentage of kindergarten and elementary–school enrollment in nonpublic schools.

tions, suggests that the public school is not satisfying some of its more affluent constituents as well as it once did.

The Results

A generation ago, greater fiscal support, lower pupil-teacher ratios, and higher levels of teacher education would have been accepted as evidence of a superior level of instruction. But since the Coleman report of 1965, which was able to identify only very small correlations between these resource characteristics and public performance on various tests of ability and achievement,[4] Americans have come to doubt whether these measures are accurate indicators of educational quality.

Increasingly, pupil performances on standardized tests have come to be viewed as the best evidence of school quality. As a result, analysts today make judgments about education quality on the basis of information that simply was not available prior to 1960. It is, however, by no means clear that this information is unequivocally superior to the data formerly examined. If tests of pupil ability were accurate measures of the quality of instruction in school, they would be extremely useful. But just as measures of per pupil expenditures do not provide direct information about how monies are used by teachers and pupils, so student performances on examinations do not provide accurate evidence of how much learning has occurred within the classroom.

Children develop their verbal and numerical skills during every waking hour of the day, whether they are at home, playing in their neighborhoods, watching television, participating in extracurricular activities, or being instructed in school. While it is thought that the intensity of learning is greater within schools, there is no proof that this is the case, and, at any rate, the school day is only five hours in length and the school year but 180 days. Attributing student performances on tests solely to the schools they attend is as inaccurate as are claims that more resources mean better schools. Even with the great advances in the social sciences over the past two decades, we still do not have ways to measure accurately the quality of instruction taking place within classrooms.

Keeping these caveats clearly in mind, I shall nonetheless present the available information on trends in educational performance during the 1970s. A trend that many have found disturbing is the decline in the average scholastic aptitude test scores of high-school seniors taking the examination as part of their college admission procedures. From 1967 to 1981, the verbal and math scores of both male and female high-school seniors declined with disconcerting regularity (see Table 2–18). Part of this decline may be attributed to the increasing percentage of minority students taking the examination and, perhaps, to the broader pool of applications to colleges more generally. Yet other evidence indicates that secondary-school students of all races and classes did less well in the late 1970s than they did in earlier years.

The most comprehensive nationwide effort to gather data on the performances of American students is that of the National Assessment of Educational Progress, which has collected comparable data at two or three different points in time in the areas of mathematics and reading. While the exact years in which the data were collected vary for each test (see Table 2–19), certain tendencies appear with sufficient regularity to permit some tentative conclusions to be drawn.

First, the data are quite consistent with the accepted stereotype that girls are better at reading and boys take more to mathematics. Significantly, differences between the sexes in mathematics ability increase as children grow older; while they are barely perceptible at age nine, they are quite pronounced at age seventeen. The stereotype seems to be a self-fulfilling prophecy. Second, differences in performances among racial groups are substantial; blacks and Hispanics do less well than whites in both reading and mathematics. For example, nine-year-old blacks scored 9.7 percent lower than whites of the same age on the 1980 reading exam. As was the case with sex differences, the differences in the performances of black and white children became greater as the

Table 2–18 Scholastic Aptitude Test Score Averages for College–Bound High–School Seniors, by Sex: United States, 1966–67 to 1980–81

	School Year				
	1966–67	1970–71	1975–76	1978–79	1980–81
Verbal scores					
Male	463	454	433	431	430
Female	468	457	430	423	418
Total	466	455	431	427	424
Mathematical scores					
Male	514	507	497	493	492
Female	467	466	446	443	443
Total	492	488	472	467	466

Sources: Department of Education, National Center for Education Statistics, *Digest of Education Statistics* (Washington, D.C.: Government Printing Office, 1980, 1982 eds.); College Entrance Examination Board, *National Report, College Bound Seniors* (New York: CEEB, 1981).

Table 2-19 National Assessment of Educational Progress in Reading and Mathematics for Ages 9, 13, and 17, by Selected Characteristics

	Reading			Mathematics	
	Mean % correct	Mean change		Mean % correct	Mean change
	1979–80	From 1974–75	From 1970–71 to 1974–75	1977–78	From 1972–73
9-year-olds	67.9	2.6	2.4	36.8	−1.3
By sex					
Male	66.0	3.0	1.4	37.0	−1.2
Female	69.7	2.3	1.0	36.7	−1.4
(% sex difference)	3.7			1.7	
By racial/ethnic group					
Hispanic	60.3	5.3	N.A.	28.6	.6
White	69.3	2.3	4.8	39.1	−2.0
Black	59.6	5.1	1.2	26.3	2.9
(% white–black difference)	9.7			12.8	
13-year-olds	60.8	0.9	0.1	50.6	−2.0
By sex					
Male	58.8	1.2	0.1	50.9	−1.8
Female	62.6	0.4	0.2	50.2	−2.3
(% sex difference)	3.8			.7	
By racial/ethnic group					
Hispanic	51.5	2.5	N.A.	36.7	−3.0
White	62.6	0.7	0.8	54.2	−2.4
Black	49.6	3.2	0.3	32.4	.6
(% white–black difference)	13.0			21.8	
17-year-olds	68.2	−0.8	−0.1	48.1	−3.6
By sex					
Male	66.9	−0.4	−0.1	49.9	−3.9
Female	69.7	−1.0	−0.1	46.4	−3.2
(% sex difference)	2.8			3.5	
By racial/ethnic group					
Hispanic	58.8	2.0	N.A.	36.0	−2.3
White	70.6	−0.6	0.4	51.0	−3.5
Black	52.2	0.1	0.2	30.9	−2.6
(% white–black difference)	18.4			20.1	

Sources: Department of Education, National Center for Education Statistics, *Digest of Education Statistics* (Washington, D.C.: Government Printing Office, 1980, 1982 eds.); National Assessment of Education Progress, *Three National Assessments of Reading: Changes in Performance* (Denver, Colo.: National Assessment of Education Progress, 1970–80, 1981 eds.).
N.A. = not available

children grew older; the differential for thirteen-year-olds was 3.3 percentage points greater than it was for nine-year-olds. Once again, social stereotypes seem to be self-fulfilling.

The differences in performance between the sexes and races are widely recognized. More interesting are the changes over time in overall performances and in the performances of various subgroups, which indicate two major trends. (See Table 2–19.) First, scores in mathematics fell significantly between 1973 and 1978. The decline, which was particularly steep among older students, is matched by a similar pattern of deterioration in science scores (not shown in the table). Reading scores, on the other hand, tended to improve steadily between 1971 and 1975 and, again, between 1975 and 1979. The main exception to this improvement in performance was among seventeen-year-olds, whose performance slipped slightly. In short, the areas of greatest concern, with the poorest performance, are at the secondary level and in mathematics and science.

Second, the differences in educational performance between blacks and whites have noticeably declined among both the younger and older age groups. Black nine-year-olds made modest gains in mathematics, while the test scores of white nine-year-olds slipped. Among thirteen-year-olds, the gap between blacks and whites narrowed in both reading and mathematics. Among seventeen-year-olds, the performances of both white and black students in mathematics and science (not shown) fell, but the slippage among white students was greater.[5] In reading, the performance of blacks improved, while white students' test scores fell. Only among nine-year-olds did white students' test score improvements outstrip those of blacks, and this is the one instance in which both groups showed significant improvements.

Consistent with the decline in the differences in educational performance between blacks and whites is the change in pupil dropout rates between 1970 and 1980. As shown in Table 2–20, in 1970 the percentage of blacks who left school prior to high-school graduation was greater than the percentage of white dropouts. But between 1970 and 1980, there was a decline in the percentage of both male and female blacks not attending school, while among whites, and especially among white males, the dropout rate *increased*. Indeed, in 1980, among sixteen- to seventeen-year-olds, the dropout rate among whites was actually higher than that for blacks. Given this reversal, it is all the more significant that the gap between black and white performance in high schools has been narrowing. It also should be pointed out that, even while fewer whites are remaining in school, the average performances of those still in the classroom have fallen.

Table 2-20 Percentage of High-School Dropouts, by Age, Race, and Sex, October 1970 and October 1978

	14- to 15-year-olds			16- to 17-year-olds			18- to 19-year-olds		
	1970	1980	% change	1970	1980	% change	1970	1980	% change
All races									
Total	1.8	1.7	−.1	8.0	8.8	.8	16.2	15.7	− .5
Male	1.7	1.3	−.4	7.1	8.9	1.8	16.0	16.9	.9
Female	1.9	2.2	.3	8.9	8.8	− .1	16.3	14.7	− 1.6
White									
Total	1.7	1.7	0.0	7.3	9.2	1.9	14.1	14.9	.8
Male	1.7	1.2	−.5	6.3	9.3	3.0	13.3	16.1	2.8
Female	1.8	2.1	.3	8.4	9.2	.8	16.3	13.8	− 2.5
Black									
Total	2.4	2.0	−.4	12.8	6.9	−5.9	31.2	21.2	−10.0
Male	2.0	1.5	−.5	13.3	7.2	−6.1	36.4	22.7	−13.7
Female	2.8	2.5	−.3	12.4	6.6	−5.8	26.6	19.8	− 6.8

Source: Department of Education, National Center for Education Statistics, *Digest of Education Statistics* (Washington, D.C.: Government Printing Office, 1980, 1982 eds.).
   a. Dropouts are persons who are not enrolled in school and who are not high-school graduates.

In Table 2-21, data from the National Assessment of Educational Progress on reading and mathematics are broken down by educational level of parents and by type of community. The results show uneven and shifting patterns. Changes in reading and mathematics scores are so inconsistent among these categories that they preclude claims that children from any particular kind of family or living in any particular area are doing exceptionally well or badly. Whatever changes are occurring in American schools are happening in cities and in rural areas, among the better-educated families and among those from families with little education. The only marked pattern in the data is the tendency for test scores to decline both generally as the pupils grow older and particularly in the science (not shown) and mathematics areas.

Multiple and competing inferences can be drawn from these findings. While it seems to be the case that students, especially white students, are learning less in their adolescent years, it is not clear whether this is due to lower educational standards in high schools; less respect for teacher authority among students; less parental instruction as children enter adulthood; increasing restlessness and anomie within a youth culture pervaded by drugs, alcohol, and premarital sex; lower expectations for success in adult life; or all of these. But while the explanations for trends are unclear, the data do suggest that educational problems are greater at the secondary than at the primary level. Since federal education policy has focused on the early years of school-

Table 2–21   National Assessment of Educational Progress in Reading and Mathematics for Ages 9, 13, and 17, by Selected Characteristics

	Reading			Mathematics	
	Mean % correct 1979–80	Mean change from 1974–75	Mean change from 1971–72 to 1974–75	Mean % change 1977–78	Mean change from 1972–73
9–year–olds	67.9	2.6	2.4	36.8	−1.3
Parental education					
No high school	60.8	2.7	−2.1	28.7	−2.3
Graduated high school	67.1	1.0	1.4	36.9	−2.4
Post high school	71.5	1.9	−0.5	42.6	−1.7
Size and type of community					
Extreme rural	66.9	4.0	2.1	32.1	−1.9
Low metropolitan	58.0	2.8	2.5	27.7	2.4
High metropolitan	73.1	1.8	−0.4	46.0	−0.7
Main big city	66.0	5.2	−2.2	33.6	−1.4
Urban fringe	69.6	1.2	0.9	41.4	−1.0
Medium city	69.0	3.5	1.6	37.8	−1.7
Small place	67.6	2.3	2.3	36.0	−1.1
13–year–olds	60.8	0.9	0.1	50.6	−2.0
Parental education					
No high school	52.9	0.4	0.5	40.3	−2.5
Graduated high school	59.5	0.1	−1.0	49.6	−2.6
Post high school	65.4	−0.6	a	58.2	−2.5
Size and type of community					
Extreme rural	58.6	1.4	a	45.2	−4.8
Low metropolitan	53.4	4.8	−2.1	36.7	2.0
High metropolitan	67.9	1.3	0.3	59.4	−4.2
Main big city	57.5	2.6	−2.1	47.0	−1.9
Urban fringe	62.8	−0.8	0.5	55.3	−0.5
Medium city	60.6	1.9	−0.5	56.6	3.2
Small place	61.1	1.0	1.4	48.9	−3.4
17–year–olds	68.2	−0.8	−0.1	48.1	−3.6
Parental education					
No high school	59.2	−1.4	0.9	37.7	−4.7
Graduated high school	65.6	−2.0	−0.7	45.5	−4.6
Post high school	73.1	−1.2	−0.7	54.1	−3.8
Size and type of community					
Extreme rural	65.1	−2.8	1.2	46.4	−2.0
Low metropolitan	59.2	0.0	−1.1	35.1	−5.7
High metropolitan	73.5	−2.5	−0.2	57.3	−2.2
Main big city	64.5	0.7	−0.3	45.7	−1.6
Urban fringe	70.8	−0.7	0.8	51.2	−2.9
Medium city	68.4	−0.9	−1.0	51.8	−2.2
Small place	68.4	−0.9	1.3	47.0	−4.2

Source: Department of Education, National Center for Education Statistics, *Digest of Education Statistics* (Washington, D.C.:   Government Printing Office, 1980, 1982 eds.); National Assessment of Education Progress, *Three National Assessments of Reading: Changes in Performance* (Denver, Colo.:   National Assessment of Education Progress, 1970–80, 1981 eds.).
a. Less than .05.

ing, and since many of the seventeen-year-olds in these studies attended schools during years when the federal role in education was only beginning, it cannot easily be shown that the problems in American education are of federal origin.

Conclusions

Some of the sources of trouble and concern in American education can be gleaned from the figures presented. Demographic changes have left the education industry in a state of decline: capital expansion has slowed, there are fewer employment opportunities, teacher salaries have fallen, educational expenditures have reached a plateau, and the percentage of the gross national product allocated to education has dropped. Coming after the rapid growth that occurred in the educational system in the 1960s, these changes are difficult to accept. They have spurred internal debate and self-criticism. Further, even though many of these changes are a function of social forces, such as changing birthrates, that are beyond the control of any particular group, it has been tempting to use scapegoats—whether these be the growing numbers of elderly, the penuriousness of the American public, or Washington bureaucrats.

But it is not just demographic changes that have generated concern about the educational system. In addition, public confidence in educational institutions seems to have waned, voter support for bond referenda has dropped, attendance at nonpublic schools has increased, and the federal government seems determined to make cuts in social services. More distressing, the achievement levels of secondary-school students are falling, especially in mathematics and science. One cannot conclude with Pangloss that in education this is the best of all possible worlds.

Yet there were many positive trends in education throughout the 1970s. Per pupil expenditures, pupil-teacher ratios, and the educational attainments of teachers all improved substantially before peaking at the end of the decade. Changes in public confidence in education have yet to be translated into substantially changed fiscal commitments to educational institutions. Moreover, recent upward shifts in non-public-school attendance must be viewed against a prior decline in non-public-school enrollments throughout the postwar period.

Nor do trends in educational achievements justify an entirely pessimistic prognosis. While secondary students are doing less well, the performance of students at the primary levels seems to have remained at least constant. If the test scores of whites have slipped somewhat, those from minority backgrounds are improving. While there has been some drop in educational quality for some groups, the system seems to be offering greater levels of educational equality.

All of these are borderline changes. Measurable differences from one period to another are at most only barely statistically significant. And it is difficult to ascertain whether they are due to changes in schooling or to changes in society. Perhaps broader changes in adolescent life are primarily responsible for declines in performance levels. Perhaps the increased employment opportunities and the rising self-confidence that the civil-rights movement gave to many black Americans are the primary causes for improved minority achievements. Nothing in these data permits the conclusion that educational institutions have deteriorated badly, and, certainly, nothing supports the claim that an increased federal role has had a fundamental effect.

Assessments of the federal role in education, therefore, must be made with the understanding that the system, although it has its problems, has withstood the shocks of the past two decades as well as any other American institution. To ascertain what the federal government should do in the future, we must examine what it has done in the past. Chapter 3 will describe the federal government's role in education prior to 1965; it will show how small sums of federal money, given with a minimum of national direction, had only a slight effect on our educational system. Chapters 4 and 5 will identify the areas in which the federal government assumed greater responsibility and gave more definite direction to local school districts after the passage, in 1965, of the Elementary and Secondary Education Act. Together, these chapters will show that, even though in the 1970s the federal government entered a terrain in which it sometimes acted awkwardly and inappropriately, its overall effect on American education has been both warranted and quite circumscribed.

3
THE TRADITION:
MINIMUM FEDERAL CONTROL

The role of the federal government in elementary and secondary education was very limited prior to 1965. There were few, if any, federal educational concerns and priorities that were not widely shared by local school districts in all parts of the country; as a result, there was little need for national direction or control. The federal government did distribute limited funds to enhance established programs. While this made for close federal, state, and local cooperation in the long run, the absence of a distinct federal purpose left these programs without adequate political support during periods of fiscal crisis and program reduction. But while federal passivity did not secure program longevity, it was probably both necessary and inevitable that the federal government's first ventures into the educational arena would have only vaguely stated expectations.

One deterrent to a more active federal role in education has been the constitutional provision reserving to the states all powers not granted to the national government. In the nineteenth century, this was understood to preclude congressional action in education. When Congress acquired an interest in education policy, it needed to find a constitutional peg on which to hook any proposed program. By and large, this hook has been the Constitution's "taxing and spending" clause. When local school districts accept federal grants-in-aid, Congress has the authority to issue instructions to guarantee their proper use. Generally speaking, even today, federal regulation in education is appropriate only insofar as it ensures the appropriate use of federal dollars or upholds due process or equal protection provisions of the Fourteenth Amendment.

The strong political opposition to federal control of public schools has been a second and even more critical reason for the limited federal role in education. After World War II, when legislation was proposed for financial aid to schools, it was strongly opposed by a broad coalition of conservative interest groups. The Chamber of Commerce, the National Association of Manufacturers, the American Legion and other veterans' groups, and patriotic associations such as the Daughters of the American Revolution were steadfast in their commitment to maintaining local control of schools. To do otherwise, they claimed, was "unnecessary, unreasonable, unsound, and dangerous to the preservation of local initiative and vitality."[1]

Both Republicans in Congress and Republican candidates for president shared at least some of the concerns of these groups. While President Eisenhower proposed federal aid for the purpose of school construction in 1955, and Richard Nixon took this same position while campaigning in 1960, both presidents, and many of their Republican colleagues on the Hill, believed that federal support for the current expenses of local school districts would endanger local control.[2] As late as 1960, the Republican platform asserted that "any large plan of federal aid to education, such as direct grants for teachers' salaries, can only lead ultimately to federal domination and control of our schools."[3]

In retrospect, it seems that conservative and Republican opposition to federal aid to education was but a surface manifestation of an underlying difficulty. Establishing a national education policy was all but impossible in a society too pluralistic to have any single national educational goal. In the 1950s, some schools had Bible reading sessions; others recognized Jewish holidays. Some schools introduced modern scientific experimental techniques; others taught what is today called creationist theory. Some schools contained the diverse mix of ethnic and racial groups that constituted big-city neighborhoods; others were rigidly segregated. Some schools had Catholic superintendents; in other places, church leaders encouraged parents to send their children to parochial institutions. Some schools had lavish facilities, equipment, and supplies; others operated on a minimal budget. Some urban comprehensive schools numbered pupils in the thousands; in many rural communities the one-room schoolhouse was still considered sufficient.

This extraordinary diversity in American education made it particularly difficult even for policymakers favorably predisposed to federal aid to education to agree on the terms for providing federal aid. While some believed that federal monies should be distributed on a per capita basis, others thought that federal aid should offset inequalities in local tax resources. While some would limit federal aid to school construction, others would extend it to augment teachers' salaries. Many were divided along racial and religious lines. Catholics were opposed to federal support for education unless parochial schools were eligible for aid; Protestant and Jewish groups, as well as many public educators themselves, were adamantly opposed to federal funding of alternatives to the "common school." The National Association for the Advancement of Colored People insisted that federal aid be given only to desegregated schools, which, in the 1950s, guaranteed a southern filibuster against any federal aid to education. It is hardly surprising that Congress regularly considered the question of general federal aid to education and just as regularly refused to do anything about it.

If general aid was not forthcoming, there were nonetheless three special aid programs for education that survived the gauntlet of group controversies. These three programs—vocational education, the National Defense Education Act, and impact aid—had vastly different origins and purposes. Passed by Congress at widely spaced intervals, they hardly comprised a national education policy. Yet a review of the context in which these programs developed, the way in which policies were implemented, the manner in which these programs maintained political support, and the mechanisms by which they were evaluated provides a baseline from which to view more recent changes in federal policy. This baseline, as will be seen, is characterized by (1) policy innovation in response to an urgent national need, (2) minimal federal direction or control of program development (aid given was in fact, if not in form, a block grant), and (3) maintenance of specialized group support to perpetuate the program after the initial sense of national crisis had passed. Examination of each of the three programs reveals this underlying pattern.

Vocational Education

Federal support of vocational programs was initiated in the midst of widespread national concern about America's capacity to compete effectively with the growing prowess of Germany. First passed in 1917, just prior to the country's entry into World War I, federal support continued on a modest scale until the early 1960s, when it was substantially revised and enlarged in response to increasing distress over rising unemployment among minority youth in urban areas. Throughout its history, the federal vocational education program has been marked by weak direction from the federal government and close integration with state and local programs. Its longevity as a federal program owes as much to the assiduous efforts of the American Vocational Association (AVA) as to its serving a distinct national mission.

Policy Development

For more than two decades prior to World War I,[4] many business, labor, and professional educators urgently demanded vocational education. But while there was nearly unanimous support for the concept of vocational education, opinion was divided as to whether it should be separate from the public schools (as many business leaders believed) or be an integral part of a comprehensive high-school program (as was preferred by labor leaders and public-school officials). In the face of the growing German threat, a compromise was finally reached—largely on the terms of public-school officials—and the Smith-Hughes Act was passed in response to the "great and crying need" for vocational education, as the congressionally established Commission on National Aid to Vocational Education expressed it.[5]

Initially, this "great and crying need" was met by annual federal expenditures of no more than $1.5 million, but the program grew steadily during the depression and war years until, after World War II, appropriations reached $36 million a year. Levels of federal fiscal support escalated rapidly after 1960, with the New Frontier-Great Society's emphasis on education. As shown in Table 3–1, which provides fiscal information on selected federal educational programs, support for vocational education programs increased in current dollars from $45 million in 1960 to $417 million in 1972 to $824 million in 1983. Even when calculated in constant dollars (see Table 3–2), these fiscal increments are dramatic for a program that previously had been a stable, routinized part of the federal system.

In its first decades, federal support to vocational education maintained a strong rural emphasis. Federal funds, which were allocated specifically for agricultural, trade, home economics, industrial, and teacher-training programs, were disproportionately distributed to rural areas.[6] This rural orientation helped sustain a base of political support for the program, despite vicissitudes of partisan allegiance and economic change. When both Herbert Hoover and Franklin Roosevelt proposed cuts in the program as part of their cost-cutting packages in the early 1930s, Congress stoutly resisted.[7] Even while the powerful chairman of the House Education and Labor Committee, Graham Barden of North Carolina, was undermining congressional consideration of general education assistance in the 1950s, he was a consistent

Table 3–1 Current Dollar Federal Expenditure for Elementary– and Secondary–Education Programs, 1960–83

Program	Fiscal Year							
	1960	1964	1968	1972	1976	1980	1982	1983
	(in millions)							
Vocational education	45.2	54.5	255.2	416.9	590.9	680.7	742.2	823.7
Federally impacted areas	258.2	334.3	506.4	648.6	598.9	821.1	456.2	480.0
NDEA	52.8	42.5	75.8	47.8	29.0	31.2[a]	–	–
Educationally deprived children	–	–	1,049.1	1,507.4	1,760.8	3,005.6	3,041.0	3,167.9
Bilingual education	–	–	–	26.0	79.5	156.4	138.1	138.1
Education for the handicapped	.7	2.5	16.8	67.9	152.1	734.5	1,068.6	1,110.2
Emergency school aid assistance	–	–	7.4	92.2	204.0	304.5	0.0	0.0
Other programs[b]	43.4	78.1	521.9	642.0	763.5	1,046.9[c]	1,447.5	1,612.1
Block grants	–	–	–	–	–	–	442.2	450.7
Total	400.3	511.9	2,432.6	3,511.8	4,178.7	6,780.9	7,335.8	7,782.7

Sources: *Education Times*, December 6, 1982, January 3, 1983; Department of Education, National Center for Education Statistics, *Digest of Education Statistics* (Washington, D.C.: Government Printing Office, 1982).
a. Estimated portion of Consolidated Program Expenditures originally funded under NDEA.
b. Includes educational research and projects, Office of Education salaries and expenses, educational personnel training (excluding higher education), educational television and broadcasting, follow–through programs, Indian education, rehabilitation services, research on the handicapped, expenditures under Consolidated Programs for purposes other than those of NDEA, and public libraries.
c. The Office of Education was merged into the new Department of Education in May 1980. Therefore, the salary data for 1980 may not be strictly comparable with those for previous years.

Table 3–2 Constant Dollar[a] Federal Expenditures for Elementary– and Secondary–Education Programs, 1960–83

Program	Fiscal Year							
	1960	1964	1968	1972	1976	1980	1982	1983
	(in millions)							
Vocational education	110.8	127.5	532.4	723.3	753.4	572.6	551.8	611.4
Federally impacted areas	632.8	782.0	486.0	1,125.3	763.6	690.6	339.2	356.3
NDEA	129.4	99.4	158.1	82.9	37.0	26.2[b]	–	–
Educationally deprived children	–	–	2,188.8	2,724.7	2,245.1	2,528.1	2,260.9	2,351.2
Bilingual education	–	–	–	45.1	101.4	131.6	102.7	102.5
Education for the handicapped	1.7	5.8	35.1	117.8	193.9	617.8	794.5	824.0
Emergency school aid assistance	–	–	15.4	160.0	260.1	256.1	–	–
Other programs[c]	106.4	182.7	1,088.9	1,113.9	1,070.9	880.6	1,076.2	1,196.5
Block grants	–	–	–	–	–	–	338.7	334.5
Total	981.1	1,197.8	4,504.7	6,093.0	5,425.4	5,703.6	5,464.0	5,776.4

Sources: *Education Times*, December 6, 1982, January 3, 1983; Department of Education, National Center for Education Statistics, *Digest of Education Statistics* (Washington, D.C.: Government Printing Office, 1982).
a. 1979 = 100.
b. Estimated portion of Consolidated Program Expenditures originally funded under NDEA.
c. Includes educational research and projects, Office of Education salaries and expenses, educational personnel training (excluding higher education), educational television and broadcasting, follow–through programs, Indian education, rehabilitation services, research on the handicapped, expenditures under Consolidated Programs for purposes other than those of NDEA, and public libraries.

supporter of vocational education.[8] Over the years, the AVA became
recognized as one of the most powerful educational interest groups in
Washington.[9] As one of its spokesmen observed:

> AVA has a reputation as being pretty effective, and it has done that through
> having its members pretty close to the important folks in Congress. It was a
> southern oriented, rural tradition kind of thing that went along real well
> with the United States Congress where the positions of power were held by
> southern Congressmen with long seniority.[10]

The politics of vocational education began to change in the early
1960s with the coming to power of a more urban-based coalition. Senator John Kennedy had promised the AVA that he would support
increased aid for vocational education during his election campaign,
but after he became president, his proposals to Congress—which
became the basis for the Vocational Education Act of 1963—were not
warmly received by the AVA or its constituent groups. The legislation,
which was passed in the torrent of legislative activity that occurred
immediately after Kennedy's assassination, attempted to shift the
focus of vocational education from serving the needs of rural, agricultural areas toward meeting the needs of urban areas, which suffered
from rapidly increasing youth unemployment. Rather than using the
old, occupational categories as the basis for the distribution of funds,
the new legislation required that monies be used for vocational training that "is realistic in light of actual or anticipated opportunities for
gainful employment."[11] In addition, the requirements for the distribution of funds within states were rewritten to encourage the redirection
of resources to urban areas. Finally, the act specified that programs be
"designed to meet the special vocational education needs of youths,
particularly youth in economically depressed communities who have
academic, socioeconomic or other handicaps."[12] When the act was
amended in 1968 and again in 1976, Congress elaborated upon its
interest in training students for occupations where market demand was
growing; in concentrating resources on the needs of special groups,
such as women, the handicapped, and minorities; and in using funds to
help those urban areas where unemployment was high. In the 1976
amendments, Congress called for a variety of planning and evaluation
mechanisms, as well as a complex system of reporting, to ensure that
states developed programs according to congressional intentions.
    Many in the vocational establishment did not embrace these
changes in program orientation, but the "vocies," as the establishment
is commonly called, nonetheless benefited from the greatly increased

level of federal assistance. In fact, the AVA proved sufficiently adaptive to be able, in 1971, with the help of Representative Roman Pucinski of Chicago, to elevate vocational education programs in the Office of Education to Bureau status.[13] Since then, Congress has continued to give strong fiscal support to vocational education.[14]

Policy Implementation

The implementation of vocational education programs has been marked by minimum national direction and maximum local control. In the programs' first decades, few federal efforts to ensure local compliance with federal policy were made. Even after the 1963 legislative changes, it was difficult to ascertain the effect of federal law on the operation of local programs. After years of operating a locally controlled vocational program with a rural orientation, state administrators did not respond readily to new federal guidelines. As a Texas official in charge of the administration of all federal programs in his state said, "Someday I would like to find out what is going on in the fourth floor vocational division."[15]

Vocational education was established at a time when federal control in education was still an anathema; even as late as 1963, legislation perpetuated patterns of local autonomy and discretion. For example, all federal vocational funds must be matched by contributions from the state or local government. If a local commitment to a particular program does not exist, then local matching funds will not be provided and the program will not be offered. Federal and state administrators are thus reluctant to insist on rigorous program requirements. Further, the federal government allocates vocational education funds to the states, which then develop their own criteria for distributing these funds among local educational agencies within the state. While Congress has specified certain criteria for intrastate distribution as part of its effort to direct funds to special constituencies and urban areas, the guidelines are expressed in such general terms that widely varying practices exist among the fifty states. In many states, vocational funds are still disproportionately allocated to rural areas.[16]

Recent research has shown that in four separate areas—planning, evaluation, sex stereotyping, and private sector involvement—federal requirements have had little local effect. For example, any state that receives federal vocational education funding is required to produce a five-year plan that, among other things, must "set out explicitly the planned uses of Federal, State, and local vocational education funds for each fiscal year of the State plan and show how these uses will enable the state to achieve these goals."[17] But as a recent analysis concluded, "local administrators concede that [state plans] are little more than documents that formally comply with the planning requirements and that they do little to shape actual policy choice."[18] In California, plans "have been largely oriented toward compliance with federal regulations rather than toward comprehensive planning."[19] As one recent study observed, "Overall implementation has fallen short of Congressional intent."[20]

Similarly, federal legislation requires that "each state shall evaluate, by using data collected, wherever possible, by statistically valid sampling techniques, each such program within the state."[21] Notwithstanding the ambitious and detailed legal requirements, most evaluations of vocational education programs in urban areas rely on impressionistic methods that in the end leave local school officials largely in control of the process.

It is true that local schools generally file an accountability report that records, for each program, the number of students by race, sex, handicap, and whether or not they are disadvantaged. External monitoring of local programs is also conducted. In Illinois, for example, state-sponsored evaluators visit each school once every five years to assess the strengths and weaknesses of the school's vocational offerings. But there is no requirement that the visitors be given information on the level of student performances. Moreover, information from on-site evaluations is not used to determine whether funding should be continued. Instead, local officials must determine whether to modify practices in light of the reviews by the evaluators.[22]

The investigators in another study of evaluation procedures found that only about half the states in their sample had any mechanism for ascertaining whether employers found students well qualified or not. Even "in those states which do collect employer follow-up data, poor response rates are an even bigger problem than they are for [student reports of their own employment experiences]; the names of employers are obtained from the completed student . . . forms, and some employers are reportedly reluctant to provide the information requested."[23]

The 1976 amendments also require local institutions "to develop and carry out such programs of vocational education within each state so as to overcome sex discrimination and sex stereotyping."[24] The legislation contains a number of specific provisions designed to achieve this objective. Local response to these provisions again proved quite limited. While local vocational administrators did not voice opposition, there is little evidence to suggest that they did much to facilitate the change. For the most part, the response was simply to open enrollment in virtually all vocational programs to members of both sexes. Although sex stereotyping in course selection has been marginally reduced as these pro forma measures were introduced, "it proved impossible to determine whether these new developments were a direct consequence of federal guidelines or whether they represented more general societal changes." However, "the paucity of local complaints about state and federal interference in this area was one indicator that little new was being asked of local officials."[25]

Finally, the 1976 amendments stipulated increased private sector involvement in local vocational education. Each recipient of federal vocational education funding is required to "establish a local advisory council to provide . . . advice on current job needs and on the relevancy of courses being offered."[26] The amendments called for broad participation on these councils, which are to include members of the general public and experts in specific vocational areas germane to the program. While such councils have, to a large extent, been created, their mere existence does not ensure valuable contacts between training programs and the private sector. Well-established, prestigious vocational institutions have long relied upon advisory councils and enjoy extensive private sector support, which the 1976 legislation only formalized. This supportive base provides curricular advisement and equipment donations to schools, as well as internships and job placements for students. Advisory councils, however, are less active in lower-quality institutions that are not so well endowed.[27]

In sum, vocational education programs were initially established when federal control was feared and rural interests were dominant. A strong vocational education interest group was organized, which developed a sizable congressional constituency, established a set of quasi-autonomous administrative structures at national and state levels, insulated program operations from all but a minimum of federal interference, and has, in general, avoided close, formal evaluation and scrutiny of its activities. While legislation in the 1960s and 1970s attempted to refocus the program to meet the needs of urban, minority youth, these enactments have only modestly altered program content and direction.

As modest as the federal impact on vocational education has been, the program profoundly shaped the expectations of both educators and public officials as to what an appropriate federal role should be and as to the way in which a politically feasible federal policy should be formulated. It became clear that policy should focus on a particular area of need, should have few federal directives, should coincide with local interests and concerns, should have the support of both parties, and, perhaps more important, should have the backing of a well-organized, highly specialized interest group. The federal government drew upon this understanding when it became concerned about the quality of education in the areas of science and mathematics.

National Defense Education Act

The National Defense Education Act (NDEA) Title III program has been the only major federal government effort whose exclusive goal was to improve the academic quality of public-school education. Its development and implementation is of special interest, inasmuch as the quality of academic education is once again a matter of national concern. Passed in the midst of a national "crisis," the NDEA, like the vocational education program, was expected to enhance the productive capabilities of the nation. The administration of Title III, like that of vocational education, minimized federal direction and allowed a maximum of local discretion in the funding of elementary- and secondary-school programs. But unlike vocational education, NDEA failed to develop a well-organized constituency that could lobby effectively on its behalf. No group comparable with the American Vocational Association was ever organized to fight for a continuation and expansion of NDEA. Neither scientists nor mathematicians, teachers nor even school boards or administrators took the cause of NDEA's Title III as their own. As a result, the purpose of the program became diffused, the nature of the aid became essentially that of a block grant, and the program was consolidated with other federal aid programs, first in 1972 under President Nixon's block grant and then again in 1981 at President Reagan's instigation. The difficulty that NDEA had in surviving as a distinct, categorical program raises the question of whether there is substantive or political justification for a federal program if it has no other purpose than to do what local school districts would do in any case. Experience suggests that federal programs may need goals and constituencies that go beyond those of local school boards and school administrators if they are to play a significant and enduring role in American education.

Policy Development

While the vocational education program concentrated on supplying manpower for the "common" occupations, NDEA was geared toward the "uncommon" ones. Passed at a time when the Soviet launching of

"Sputnik" raised questions about the scientific capabilities of the United States, the legislation focused on curricula for science, mathematics, and foreign languages. While much of the legislation focused on the needs of higher education, Title III authorized funds for the purchase of equipment, supplies, and minor remodeling for elementary and secondary schools.[28] Given the fanfare with which it was launched, the middle-class constituency it supposedly served, and its apparent relevance to the nation's defense capabilities, it is surprising that NDEA did not expand and develop over the next two decades in the way so many other educational programs did. While it grew from a less than $53 million program in 1960 to a more than $75 million program in 1968, the NDEA allocation declined in subsequent years, falling to $29 million in 1976 and finally becoming consolidated with other programs in 1980. (See Tables 3–1 and 3–2.)

At the same time that expenditures were falling, the purposes of NDEA were becoming increasingly diffuse. In the beginning, support was limited to programs in science, mathematics, and foreign languages, but in 1964 Congress added programs in history, civics, geography, English, and reading; in the following year, programs in economics, the arts and humanities, and even industrial arts were included. Thus, the distribution of funds among subject areas altered dramatically between the early 1960s and the mid-1970s. As shown in Table 3–3, the percentage of funds allocated for the sciences dropped from 74 to 18 percent, while reading and social studies, which received nothing in early years, were recipients of more than 40 percent of NDEA monies in 1976. By that time, almost any subject could have been said to be important for improving the defense capabilities of the nation.

This diffusion in its purpose made NDEA ripe for consolidation with other educational programs. Although Congress generally resisted the block-grant proposals of the Nixon administration, it agreed to consolidation when program purposes could not be clearly articulated and when supporting constituencies were weak. Since NDEA funding helped purchase equipment and supplies for a wide variety of school subjects, there was little justification for its separate existence, and, therefore, it was lumped together with such programs as library services, guidance and counseling, and general aid to state departments of education.

NDEA's limited fiscal growth and diffusion of purpose were in part due to the fact that it lacked a well-defined, supportive political constituency. The scientific community was more concerned with sustaining federal support for ongoing research than with training the next generation of scientists. Colleges and universities were abandoning

Table 3–3   Percentage Distribution of Federal NDEA Funds among Subject Areas

Subject Areas	Fiscal Year	
	1959–62	1976
Science	73.8%	18.2%
Mathematics	8.6	9.0
Foreign languages	17.6	1.7
English and reading	–	26.7
Social studies	–	14.7
Arts and humanities	–	12.2
Industrial arts	–	9.1
Audio visual libraries	–	8.4
Total	100.0%	100.0%
Total (n)	$140,400,000[a]	$12,700,000[b]

Sources: Department of Health, Education, and Welfare, Office of Education, *Report on the National Defense Education Act, Fiscal Years 1961 and 1962* (Washington, D.C.: Government Printing Office, 1963), and Office of Planning, Budgeting and Evaluation, *Annual Report on Programs Administered by the U.S. Office of Education, Fiscal Year 1977* (Washington, D.C.: Government Printing Office, 1978).
a. Paid by the Office of Education to the states and territories for equipment and minor remodeling up to June 30, 1962.
b. "Program Acquisition" expenditures under NDEA Title III during fiscal 1976. These figures do not include expenditures made under ESEA, IV–B.

their language requirements, thereby weakening the demand for foreign language instruction at the secondary-school level. Since NDEA funds were not to be used for teachers' salaries, neither the National Education Association nor the American Federation of Teachers had a major stake in the program. Its only constituency was the school boards, school superintendents, and state departments of education that used NDEA monies to purchase materials and equipment.

While these local school interests supported NDEA, they also sought to minimize its restrictions and to maximize the range of activities that could be funded. In the early 1960s, when NDEA was still the major new federal program in education, it received only mixed local reviews. As a scholar noted at the time, "Both the Impacted Areas Act and the NDEA had been supported with warmth and enthusiasm by many professional educators, public officials, and interested laymen. However, both these acts clearly held second place to [a] more general bill. . . ."[29] The American Association of School Administrators faulted the NDEA for being "cumbersome, expensive to administer, characterized by too much red tape, and, in several respects, it exerts [a level of] control and federal direction over the public school curriculum which is unsound in terms of national and state policy."[30] In the words of one superintendent who participated in a national round table on the law, "The only way we can have federal aid without federal control is to grant a lump sum to each state and let the educational authorities in each state determine how they're going to spend it. . . . I'm opposed to earmarking, period!"[31] Views such as these were the basis for insistence by the Council of Chief State School Officers that NDEA be broadened to include many more subjects than just science, mathematics, and foreign languages.

Policy Implementation

When there were no countervailing pressures, local school officials were generally successful in securing the program they wanted. Not only did Congress broaden the purposes of the law, but more important, the Office of Education, in implementing the legislation, exerted almost no control over the ways in which federal dollars could be spent. If the vocational education programs had been given only the loosest direction by federal officials, NDEA was hardly administered at all. While the Office of Education prepared a twenty-page form that explained to state education agencies (SEAs) the way in which their proposed plans should be submitted for approval, the requirements set forth were hardly stringent. Further, the Office of Education instructed its employees:

> . . . always remember that the States and local communities have primary responsibility for education and must retain full control over it. Therefore, do not construe any part of this Act to authorize you or any of your employees to exercise any direction over the curriculum, program of instruction, administration, or personnel of any educational institution or school system.[32]

Accordingly, the federal government proved very receptive to the state plans submitted. In the first year of the program, "More than 90 percent of the states had 90 percent or more of their requested projects, measured in dollar terms, approved."[33] This high acceptance rate is particularly significant, given the vague, general character of the plans. In the words of one well-informed observer, the SEAs ". . . in their plans mostly stuck to bland and general descriptions of programs, priorities and standards. Some came close to parroting the illustrations sent from Washington. . . . No state intended to embarrass the Commissioner or to tie itself too closely to specifics."[34]

The financial arrangements for distributing NDEA funds reinforced the tendency toward loose federal control. The distribution formula determined allocations among the states, but the SEAs had the responsibility for allocating funds among local school districts. Since funds were distributed on a 50 percent matching-grant basis, only those local school districts or states willing to match federal funds with their own participated in the program. Under these circumstances, federal regulations could not be particularly onerous. The matching-grant requirement also meant that a disproportionately high percentage of the funds went to larger and more wealthy districts, where administrative and fiscal resources were greater.[35]

Permissiveness at the national level was matched by the flexibility of state departments of education, which traditionally allowed local school districts a good deal of autonomy in their use of fiscal resources. Even in those states in which SEAs wished to provide a degree of leadership there were few signs of central direction and control. As reported in the early years of the program, "the Title III program has effectively accomplished its objectives without impairing the traditional pattern of local initiative with state support."[36]

Loose central control was coupled with lack of interest in substantive evaluation of the program's effectiveness. To the best of my knowledge, no study of the effects of NDEA on student performances in science, mathematics, or any other subject area has ever been undertaken, and there is no record of any systematic, experimental design research to identify the effects of any specific curricular materials purchased with NDEA funds. Any difference in student performances between schools participating in the program and those not participating is yet to be determined. While studies of this kind were not an integral part of government programming in the late 1950s and early 1960s when NDEA was established, even when these studies became fashionable in the 1970s, they were not applied to NDEA. Instead, nonevaluation has been rationalized by the claim that "evaluation on a nationwide basis of any program is difficult since the necessary *before* bench marks are seldom available for comparison with the *after* results."[37]

Assessments of the administration and management of NDEA programs are also scarce. In 1972, the Office of Education admitted that at the state level, "staff limitations prevented extensive monitoring."[38] State officials relied primarily on written reports from the staffs of local education agencies and on a few site visits. Thus, in its 1972 review of the "degree of success" NDEA had "in achieving program objectives," the Office of Education relied upon nothing more than testimonials and anecdotes. For example, it included in its annual report the information that in New Jersey, "state consultants (in mathematics) report that the availability of better materials and equipment has had a favorable effect on teacher attitudes."[39] It also reported that in an "evaluation of the reading program" in Nebraska, one student wrote, "This is the best year I've had in school. I don't like books much yet, but I don't hate them. I like to use the electrical equipment."[40] These annual reviews—only two of which have ever been released by the Office of Education—were little more than public relations documents.

A Southern Illinois University study, released in 1969, focused on program management; it did not assess state plan effectiveness.[41] More recently, a much higher quality study by Rand attempted to identify the consequences of consolidating NDEA with other educational programs. The study pointed out that consolidation allowed for the continuation of permissiveness in program operations and encouraged disproportionate participation by wealthier districts. The Rand study, which focused on administrative activities, did not examine the substantive effects the NDEA program might have had.[42]

Despite the looseness with which NDEA was administered, there were protests about excessive administration and red tape. From the very beginning, local administrators complained that procedures for filing project proposals, for having them approved, and for collecting reimbursement funds were "burdensome." One analyst estimated "the cost in California of simply writing and typing NDEA Title III projects for one year—1967—to be $1,290,000, or $10.75 per page."[43] After NDEA was consolidated with other educational programs, coordination and control also became a problem for some local schools; the complaint often heard was that teachers do not know "what has been ordered for their schools until the materials arrive."[44] These complaints notwithstanding, NDEA was a federal program developed and implemented almost exactly along the lines preferred by school officials.

In sum, NDEA presents a puzzle for those called upon to think about federal education policy for the 1980s. The program provided general aid for academically oriented school activities; it did not focus on the needs of any specific constituency; it was administered in such a way as to give great autonomy and flexibility to local officials; and no formal evaluations of its operations were ever made. Some observers now believe that the program simply supplied materials and equipment that local districts would otherwise have purchased out of their own funds.[45] Yet even though the program became, in effect, a block grant for local school districts, it seemed to have lost its sense of purpose and, with weak political support, was phased out altogether in 1981. One possible conclusion is that, if a federal program that has no other purpose than to do what local school districts would do in any case, it has little reason for being. All it accomplishes is to add to the administrative complications of state and local officials. Any federal effort to enhance the quality of academic programs, therefore, must develop identifiable goals and constituencies that clearly supplement those of local school boards.

Aid to Federally Impacted Areas

If NDEA disappeared, in part, for lack of a definable focus, the same might have been expected of the federal "impact aid" program. Of all the categorical programs currently authorized by Congress, it is the one that comes the closest to being a "block grant." Impact aid monies can be used by local school districts for any educational purpose, and the regulations governing this program are minimal. Since its purpose is so poorly defined, the program has periodically encountered political difficulties. Indeed, virtually every president has questioned the value of the program and has sought to cut its appropriation. Only strong lobbying efforts in Congress by those school districts that are the program's primary beneficiaries have kept impact aid an ongoing program.

Policy Development

Impact aid was created as a temporary program during World War II to assist school districts overwhelmed by the arrival of military personnel in areas of the country that were primary centers of wartime activity. It was reestablished and its scope broadened in 1950, when two subcommittees of the House Committee on Education and Labor jointly reported that the federal presence was creating severe burdens in many other school districts. President Truman proposed, and, shortly after the outbreak of the Korean War, Congress enacted, legislation to assist such districts. In separate pieces of legislation, aid was provided for both current expenses and for the construction of additional school facilities, particularly needed at that time because of burgeoning school enrollments. Two different levels of assistance were established: one—the higher rate—was based on the number of pupils in a school district whose parents both lived and worked on federal property (i.e., in most cases, children of military personnel); the other—a lower rate—was based on the number of children whose parents either lived or worked on federal property.

The president and the Office of Management and Budget have found little justification for continuing the impact aid program, as it can no longer be said that federal activities constitute a "burden" for local school districts. To the contrary, many states and localities eagerly bid for the location of a new space agency, defense installation, or federal regional facility, as the establishment of a federal program in a community generally improves the area's employment opportunities, provides a "shot in the arm" for the local economy, and increases local property values and tax revenues. Provision of impact aid to local schools is only an added benefit, given to those seemingly least in need of it. As President Kennedy observed when he reluctantly signed this program into law in 1961:

> . . . more undesirable is the continuation for two more years of the current aid-to-impact-areas program, which gives more money to more schools for more years than either logic or economy can justify. This Administration recommended a reduction in the cost of this program, an increase in its eligibility requirements and local participation, its extension for only one year instead of two, and its eventual absorption in a general aid-to-education program. The rejection of all these requirements highlights the air of utter inconsistency which surrounds this program.[46]

In spite of presidential resistance, the legislation has remained popular in Congress, which has been lobbied assiduously by the National Association of Impacted Districts. Over 4,000 school districts—located in virtually every congressional district—have become beneficiaries of the program.[47] During the past three decades, program eligibility has gradually been extended. In 1956, for example, children of military personnel on active duty away from home were made eligible; in 1958, restrictions on monies to larger school districts were eased, Indian children became eligible, and any child with a parent in federal employ was counted for purposes of aid distribution. In 1963, Washington, D.C., schools became beneficiaries; in 1965, construction assistance was made available to those areas suffering a "major disaster"; in 1967, the definition of "minimum school facilities" was broadened; in 1970, children living in federally subsidized, low-rent housing were included in the program. In 1974, and again in 1978, Congress attempted to organize these changes into a systematic statement on eligibility, which in the end further extended the benefits and introduced new complexities into eligibility requirements.

All of these complex, continuing extensions of eligibility by Congress helped sustain legislative support for the law. As shown in Table 3–4, in every year since 1970, Congress appropriated hundreds of millions of dollars more for impact aid than the president requested. But while Congress maintained the impact aid program, executive resistance placed definite limits on its size. Table 3-2 shows that, while many other educational programs were expanding, the impact aid program declined in constant dollars; under the Reagan administration, impact aid has been one of the most severely cut educational programs.

Policy Implementation

The inability of impact aid to maintain a political base of support is probably related to the diffuseness of the program's educational purpose. While eligibility requirements for the funds are quite specific, Congress issued few guidelines as to how the assistance was to be used by local school boards once allocated. In order to receive assistance for capital expenditures, local districts have to demonstrate a need for expansion, but there is no constraint on the purposes for which funds

Table 3–4   Federal Funding to Impact Aid, 1970–83, in Constant Dollars[a]

Fiscal Year	Budget Requested by the Administration (in thousands)	Amount Appropriated by the Congress (in thousands)
1970	$377,980	$1,122,097
1971	761,335	987,170
1972	763,404	1,062,806
1973	704,472	1,113,995
1974	431,137	899,123
1975	459,423	885,657
1976	339,453	867,774
1977	389,309	949,914
1978	439,670	890,470
1983	212,923	356,258

Sources: *Congressional Quarterly Almanac* (1969), p. 547; (1970), p. 261; (1971), p. 205; (1972), p. 874; (1973), p. 157; (1974), p. 110; (1975), p. 785; (1976), p. 791; (1977), pp. 297–98; (1978), p. 106; (1979), p. 237; *Education Week,* January 26, 1983.
a. 1979 = 100.

earmarked for current expenditures can be used. The initial legislation required that:

> In the administration of this Act, no department, agency, officer, or employee of the United States shall exercise any direction, supervision, or control over the personnel, curriculum, or program of instruction of any school or school system of any local or state educational agency.[48]

While the impact aid program has remained largely faithful to this charge, some federal regulation has been inevitable. In order to obtain aid for constructing new facilities, local school districts must show that children within their districts lack minimum school facilities. Districts with "unhoused" pupils, or districts that require funding to make major building repairs for the safety of school children, or districts that propose facilities that would enable them to offer a "contemporary educational program," are eligible for assistance.[49] Each school district submitting requests for funds for more than one project is required to rank the projects in order of priority.

But while decisions on capital expansion require federal administrators to pass educational judgment, monies for operating programs are allocated without regard to their use. A formula, based on the number of eligible pupils, is used to allocate funds among school districts. Only two exceptions have occurred: First, extra funds for handicapped children could be obtained if these students were enrolled in special programs. Second, money available under a provision that granted eligibility for impact aid to pupils living in public housing was to be used for compensatory educational purposes. This second stipulation on the use of impact aid funds was withdrawn in 1978.

Otherwise, federal regulations on impact aid have been limited to specifying the procedures to be used to estimate the number of pupils eligible for assistance. For example, regulations try to define what constitutes being employed on federal property, what evidence is needed to establish that a child resides with a parent who has some connection with the federal government, and the way in which average, daily public-school attendance is to be determined.[50] Over the years, such specifications have lengthened the impact aid application form from five to seventeen pages, and the number of program administrators has increased. Nonetheless, even in 1977 this vast federal aid program was administered by only sixty-two professionals in the Office of Education.[51]

Like NDEA, impact aid has no constituency beyond the local school districts receiving the program's funds. Only local school districts are interested in program operations, and as a result, federal regulations are minimal and have virtually no impact on local education practice. Also like NDEA, the impact aid program lacks justification for federal funding. The allotment of federal aid to school districts seems more a function of historical accident and congressional compromise than the product of a coherent understanding of a proper federal role in education. Diffuse political support in Congress may help such programs survive, but they are under constant pressure to justify their existence. Over time, they seem to wither away, receiving declining proportions of the educational dollar.

Conclusions

The vocational education, NDEA, and impact aid programs are survivors of an earlier epoch, when federal control was widely abhorred, and civil-rights questions had only marginal political significance. Even in the early 1960s, when these programs distributed sizable funds—amounting to more than 4 percent of all educational expenditures—they had little more than a fiscal impact. There was minimal federal regulation and maximal local autonomy in the workings of each of these programs. As a result, the programs have been popular among local school boards, school administrators, and state departments of education. This local popularity has encouraged Congress to support consistently the continuation of these programs, even in the face of, in some cases, strong executive resistance.

Nonetheless, the sources of the programs' popularity—the flexibility and autonomy with which the Office of Education has allowed school districts to operate these programs—has also been their weakness—the absence of any distinct federal goal or purpose and, correspondingly, the lack of any significant political constituency other than local school officials themselves. Since elementary and secondary education is primarily a state and local responsibility, there must be a justification for federal action. But defense of federal action in these three program areas has become increasingly difficult. Clearly, state and local governments, which pay for more than 90 percent of the costs of occupational training and an even higher percentage of the cost of academic instruction, would continue to provide both vocational education and education in mathematics and science, even if Congress were to eliminate its programs in these areas. And although the more than 4,000 school districts that have grown dependent on impact aid would have to find alternative sources of fiscal support should this program be eliminated, it is hardly clear that most would suffer any greater hardships than those endured by the thousands of school districts that are not said to be "impacted."

Federal programs without a clear federal purpose may survive either through sheer inertia or through the building of alliances on Capitol Hill. But since these programs lack luster and elan, in the long run they tend to wither away. As a program, NDEA has disappeared altogether, and impact aid dollars have been cut back dramatically. Certainly, if these remained the only federal programs in education, there would be little reason not to consolidate them into a block grant containing the most minimal federal guidelines.

4
THE REDEFINITION:
FEDERAL PURSUIT OF EQUALITY

Until 1965, the federal government promoted educational programs that were basically consistent with state and local objectives. Federal regulation was minimal, and local governments were generally satisfied with program administration because they were asked to do little more than they would do in any event. With the passage of the Elementary and Secondary Education Act (ESEA) in 1965, the situation changed markedly. Federal involvement increased, based on the premise that local school districts had failed to support adequately social equity and equality of educational opportunity. The federal government assumed the responsibility, not for helping local school districts, but for helping certain groups in the population that had been inadequately served. This change introduced new complexity into the federal role in education. On the one hand, the federal government had taken on a distinct mission, which resulted in the steady growth of federal expenditures over the following decade and a half. On the other hand, federal policymakers did not fully appreciate the fact that the processes of teaching and learning are art forms, not easily reduced to a set of procedures that can be scientifically determined and dictated from on high. The most successful policies, it was belatedly learned, were those restricted to assuring equitable allocation of tangible resources: how these resources were to be used within schools was a decision best left to the discretion of policymakers at the local level.

The complexities of intergovernmental relations in the area of education increased markedly after 1965. The federal government no longer assumed that local governments could operate federal programs without much supervision, became suspicious that funds were being diverted from statutory purposes, and launched a wide variety of studies and evaluations to ascertain program impact. Instead of harmonious, supportive relations, conflicts and controversies began to pervade federal education policy. Instead of broad support by general educational groups, a wide range of new organizations with specific interests in particular education policies vigorously backed the new federal programs.

The next two chapters will trace the development of this new federal role in elementary and secondary education. Chapter 4 will address the first, largest, and most complex of the new federal policies, Title I of the Elementary and Secondary Education Act, which not only gave the federal government a new distinct role, but which also inspired the formulation of succeeding programs. Chapter 5 will examine three of the most important of these succeeding programs—bilingual education, the Emergency School Aid Act, and education for the handicapped.

The Elementary and Secondary Education Act

Policy Development

ESEA was the first major piece of legislation signed by President Lyndon Johnson after his landslide election in 1964. Passed by Congress at the height of national attention to civil rights, poverty, and social reform, the legislation expressed fundamental concern for the needs of minorities and the poor. In its opening statement of purpose, ESEA promised to "expand and improve . . . education programs . . . which meet the special needs of educationally deprived children."[1] The major section of the law, Title I, allocated funds to school districts with concentrations of children from low-income families; these funds were advanced in response to local initiatives. This program has remained the central pillar of federal education policy. Since its initial passage, the law has been reauthorized three times (in 1970, 1974, and 1978). But the additions and modifications made on these occasions generally did not detract from the law's original reform-minded purpose; instead, they tended to clarify and elaborate Congress's intentions. In 1981, many of these additions and modifications were eliminated or replaced by more vaguely worded language such as had existed originally. The effects of this latest change are yet to be ascertained.

As shown in Tables 3–1 and 3–2, compensatory education programs account for nearly one-half the appropriations made directly by the

Department of Education to elementary and secondary education. Thus, any evaluation of federal education policy must, above all, be an assessment of compensatory education programs. Given its size and breadth, Title I can be said to represent the core of this federal education policy. Since its initial passage, it has enjoyed fairly consistent fiscal support. While it did not expand rapidly, as its proponents initially hoped, the size of the program gradually increased, as measured in current dollars, and until 1980, held its own even in constant dollars.

The discussion of compensatory education that follows will focus on two separate aspects of the program. The first, resource allocation among school districts (the territorial aspect), which is of great interest to Congress, deals with the legislative formulas that portion monies among the various school districts. At issue is the equity of the distribution of fiscal resources among states and localities. The second (the programmatic aspect) deals with the way funds are used by local school districts once federal fiscal allocations have been made. In this area, the federal government takes an interest in the extent to which federal resources are focused specifically on the educational needs of disadvantaged children. Of particular concern are the level of contributions made by local governments, the nature of the services they provide, and the manner in which they identify eligible children.

Territorial Issue:
Resource Allocation among School Districts

Congress is a legislative body whose members have a special interest in the effects any federal program will have on the districts from which they are elected. Consequently, they are tempted to ask of any federal program the following questions: How much money is going to my district? Will my district get more or less than it did last year? Which of the proposed formulas will do my district the most good? The answers to these questions can often be given with a good deal of precision, especially since computers have greatly increased information-processing capacities. As a result, the district-by-district impact of federal fiscal policies often becomes central to policymaking on Capitol Hill.

The significance that Congress attaches to these territorial interests is manifested in a variety of ways. In the first place, for many programs, allocation of funds among districts is specified with extraordinary exactitude. While Congress leaves numerous programmatic aspects of the programs it approves to the discretion of the administrative agency in charge, often no discretion at all is allowed in the district-by-district allocation of funds. The bulk of Title I funds, for example, is allocated according to a strict formula that states exactly how much weight is to be given to each factor in the fiscal equation. Second, Congress attends so carefully to the district-by-district impact of its policies that it frequently amends them as political majorities shift. In the case of ESEA, a strong northeastern and southern bias evident in the first years of the program was modified in the early 1970s, when midwestern and western influences gained in strength, only to be modified a third time as political currents changed again. Third, Congress prizes most highly those evaluations of its programs that focus on their district-by-district impact. For example, the National Institute of Education conducted a massive study of Title I, which was extravagantly praised by Congress in 1977. Although the analysis provided comparatively little information on the effects of the program on student performances, it supplied an appreciative Congress with a detailed analysis of the impact of different funding formulas on each district.[2]

In light of the above, it is not surprising that the allocation of ESEA resources has been a matter of continuing legislative debate. Originally, the formula for distributing these funds was based on two major considerations: the number of children from low-income families living within a school district and the average cost per pupil of education within that state. While the formula seemed consistent with the objective of serving disadvantaged children, Republican critics argued that some of the school districts that would receive the most resources were fiscally well endowed. They proposed instead that the program offset existing inequalities in local fiscal resources. But the Democratic majority prevailed, perhaps because the funding formula tended to favor large central cities and the rural South, the two areas of greatest Democratic strength.

Within two years following passage of the legislation, efforts were made to modify the formula to shift funding away from the highly industrialized Northeast. In 1967, for example, southern congressmen demonstrated (by means of a computer simulation) that southern states, which spent relatively low amounts on education, would greatly benefit if the resource allocation formula were based on the average national cost per pupil instead of the statewide average. Accordingly, some accommodation in the funding formula was made. After a number of program evaluations revealed that wealthier districts were receiving more Title I funds, further changes were made in the course of the reauthorization of 1970, which "generally shifted the aid from wealthier urban states to the poorer, rural ones."[3]

In 1974, the debate centered on the weight that should be given to the number of children receiving public welfare assistance. Since wealthier, more industrialized states tended to have the least restrictive welfare practices, it was argued in Congress that "the wealthier a state, the more likely it is that it will . . . be able to add AFDC [Assistance to Families with Dependent Children] children under Title I."[4] While New York Representative Shirley Chisholm argued that reducing the weight of this provision of the formula "represents a retreat from the intent of Title I to assist those areas with large concentrations of needs,"[5] the distribution formula was further modified. Once Republicans gained greater strength at both ends of Pennsylvania Avenue, the type of arguments they originally made in 1965 became much more persuasive.

By 1978, when the legislation came up for reauthorization for a third time, Democrats were once again in political ascendance, and new changes in the distribution formula were proposed. A study by the National Institute of Education had shown that little was to be gained from, and great complexity would be introduced by, changing the formula from consideration of the incidence of children from low-income families to consideration of the incidence of children whose educational performances were deficient. Another study, which was well received in the new political climate, argued that "the fiscal and educational needs of the high expenditure metropolitan states and their major cities deserve greater consideration than they received from Congress" in 1974.[6] As a result, in a formula made increasingly complicated by the various amendments that had gradually accrued, the large cities regained some of their initial advantage. But even before these amendments took effect, the distribution of funds had favored the northeastern cities and southern rural areas, the original winners in the allocation contest (see Table 4–1).

Had the federal government decided to administer its aid to education through a block-grant program, such as that proposed by the Nixon administration in the early 1970s, the geographic distribution of resources would have been very different. Instead of distributing the monies directly to local school districts, funds would be allocated among the fifty states, which would then make within-state allocations. Suburban areas and small towns would very likely have gained at the expense of central cities. In fact, the Nixon administration's general revenue-sharing plan, which replaced many categorical programs in noneducational policy areas, had shifted federal dollars away from central cities toward a wide variety of government bodies in small communities and rural areas.[7]

In part, congressmen from urban areas strongly defend categorical programs in order to maintain the financial assistance currently received in the districts they represent. When Congress was consider-

Table 4-1 Title I Allocations, by Region and Place Type, per School-Aged Child, 1975–76

	Region			
Place Type	Northeast	North Central	South	West
Central city	$58.24	$38.02	$40.81	$31.58
Large	67.03	44.94	41.29	33.79
Other	37.11	24.94	40.12	26.83
Suburbs	17.77	14.22	26.42	22.80
Urban	17.52	13.02	21.34	21.49
Rural	18.53	17.32	35.76	30.12
Nonmetropolitan	29.18	27.46	54.14	34.53
Urban	27.80	20.39	44.95	28.94
Rural	29.89	31.63	58.71	39.05

Source: National Institute of Education, *Title I Funds Allocation: The Current Formula* (Washington, D.C.: Department of Health, Education, and Welfare, 1977), p. 1112.

ing the administration's proposals in connection with the 1974 reauthorization, one urban Democratic congressman questioned the Milwaukee school superintendent as follows:

> I am going to ask you a hypothetical question and ask you at the end to indicate to me in which of these two situations you feel there is more local control and local direction. . . . Assume one, a Title I program administered by the Federal government where the money goes to the local school district on a formula basis. Guidelines set out the kinds of programs you are supposed to have. Illustration A. . . . Illustration B. Money goes from the Federal government to the state government to the local government and the programs to be followed by the local government and the programs to be followed by the local school districts are prescribed by the state and you are told what you can do with that money by the state. . . . Now under which of those two situations is there more or less local control and local direction? . . . [The school superintendent responded:] I think I would be inclined . . . to go with the first. . . . I am getting about 15 cents on the dollar from the state [while] the average from state support for other districts in the state is about 30 percent; it is over double.[8]

A Detroit administrator also observed, "We want to be secure in the funds and in the ability for us to mount these programs. . . . We feel secure under the ESEA."[9] Significantly, the question was posed in terms of external "control" of local programming, but the participants were largely concerned about the effects of the two different funding mechanisms on the geographical distribution of financial aid.

A "correct" or "just" allocation formula is an elusive goal. It can be argued that federal aid should offset inequalities in state and local fiscal resources. It also can be argued that the labor and other costs of education are so much higher in urban areas that federal aid must compensate these communities at higher rates. It can be argued, as in Title I, that the needs of low-income children are so special that additional funds are required wherever they are concentrated. Or it can be argued that a flat grant for every pupil in each and every school district, regardless of the needs of its children or the resources of the local property tax, will lead to the least federal interference. But whatever rationale for federal aid is selected, the resulting formula will have varying consequences for different geographical regions, and the representatives from those regions are likely to react accordingly.

Programmatic Issues:
The Use of ESEA Resources by Local School Districts

While members of Congress are especially interested in the allocation of resources among states and localities, many educators, educational interest groups, members and staffs of key legislative committees, and the Department of Education itself are particularly interested in the allocation of resources within school districts. When ESEA was initially passed, congressional intentions with respect to educational programming were vague, probably deliberately so. But in the 1970s, Congress was encouraged by new policy-specific interest groups to give increasingly clear direction to ESEA. Over time, a policy that might have been little more than a general aid program along the lines of impact aid, became a categorical program with well-defined policy intentions.

Originally, Title I represented a compromise between federal policymakers, who had reforms in mind, and traditional educational interest groups, who would have preferred a program without strings attached. Both sides to the debate had resources they could muster. The massive congressional majority that accompanied the Johnson landslide had so consolidated power within the White House that Francis Keppel, commissioner of education, with his staff and a number of White House aides, was able to develop a comprehensive piece of legislation that passed Congress without amendment. It took into account both the work of a presidential task force, which had recommended that federal aid be used to reform educational institutions, and Keppel's own ideas.

While the legislation was written within the executive branch, rele-

vant outside political interests were not ignored. Catholics were reas-
sured that Title I was for disadvantaged children, no matter what
school they attended, and that Title II allowed the distribution of curricular materials to nonpublic schools. Public-school officials were told
that the program was essentially a general aid program to public education. Although state departments of education would have little
influence over Title I resource allocations, they were given substantial
grants in Title V to strengthen their administrative staffs. Southerners
were told that nothing in the act specifically called for desegregation
and that southern states would be well treated by the distribution
formula. Civil-rights groups were delighted that the purpose of the program was defined in poverty-related terms. In typical Johnsonian style,
consensus was fashioned among a complexity of interests that previously had defeated all other large-scale federal aid programs.

To paper over differences, the legislation was ambiguous in many
respects. For example, the amount of resources to be given to nonpublic schools was left to state and local discretion, and on the whole,
nonpublic schools benefited from the program to a much lesser extent
than they had anticipated. Only 43 percent of the districts that receive
Title I monies provide services to children from low-income families
attending nonpublic schools.[10] Southerners discovered that ESEA,
when coupled with Title VI of the Civil Rights Act, passed just the year
before, provided the most powerful tool for school desegregation the
region had ever experienced. In order to become eligible for Title I
funds, the South desegregated at a faster rate in the following five years
than any other part of the country ever had before or has since.

The legislation also was ambiguous about the extent to which the
federal intent was to focus on the needs of children from low-income
families. On the one side, control over programmed administration
remained in local hands. This law, like the impact aid legislation,
stated flatly that:

> Nothing contained in this Act shall be construed to authorize any depart-
> ment, agency, officer, or employee of the United States to exercise any direc-
> tion, supervision or control over the curriculum, program of instruction,
> administration or personnel of any educational institution or school sys-
> tem. . . . [11]

Applications for support, moreover, were to be submitted to state
departments of education, just as National Defense Education Act
(NDEA) applications had been handled. Most of the funds were to be
distributed on a formula basis, thereby implying that local districts had
a "right" to a certain fixed sum. But on the other side, certain features

of the law placed definite constraints on local school districts. They had to submit proposals for funding, which were to be "designed to meet the special educational needs of educationally deprived children" and were to be "of sufficient size, scope and quality to give reasonable promise of substantial progress toward meeting these needs." The law also required that "effective procedures, including provision for appropriate objective measurements of educational achievement . . . be adopted for evaluating . . . the effectiveness of the programs."[12] Various reports and evaluations were to be submitted to demonstrate compliance with these requirements.

The Office of Education had difficulty in securing compliance with these provisions in the first years of the program, a problem discussed in the following section. Accordingly, with each reauthorization of ESEA, Congress developed more stringent guidelines designed to ensure closer adherence to its policy objectives. For example, Congress not only rejected the Nixon proposals for a more general educational aid program in 1974 but called for "independent evaluations" of programs that "measure the impact of programs and projects," and publication of "standards for evaluation of program or project effectiveness." In 1978, Congress went much further in specifying the ways in which Title I monies could be used. While many of the new provisions only concretized in legislative form regulations that had already become part of the Office of Education's standard operating procedures, they now had the force of law. Among the new provisions, the following were the most important:

1. *Concentration of services.* All districts must rank their schools according to the degree of concentration of children attending from low-income families. ESEA-supported services provided to a school with a lesser concentration of students from low-income families must be provided to all those schools with a greater concentration of students from low-income families.

2. *Maintenance of effort.* The local school district, drawing on state and local resources, must maintain the level of fiscal support it provided to eligible schools in the penultimate fiscal year.

3. *Supplementation, not supplantation, of services.* ESEA monies can be used only for services in addition to those that would have been provided to participating students in the absence of a federal program.

4. *Comparability of services.* Students participating in the ESEA program must also be receiving services, from state and local sources, that are comparable with those offered to students not receiving services under Title I.

5. *Individualized plans.* Districts are "encouraged" to develop for

each child aided under the act an individualized plan agreed upon by the local educational agency, the teacher, a parent, and, when appropriate, the child.

6. *Advisory council involvement.* The advisory councils, consisting of parents of children receiving services under the act, shall have access to relevant information and opportunities to participate in a training program; the effectiveness of these advisory councils shall be evaluated.

7. *Evaluations.* The program must be evaluated by independent contractors and by local school districts, which are to perform this service according to a set of standard models supplied by the commissioner of education.

While exemptions to these rules were allowed in particular circumstances, these regulations, together with other requirements, defined much more clearly and explicitly than did the original legislation Congress's intention to concentrate ESEA monies on educationally disadvantaged pupils from low-income families.

A variety of forces facilitated this drive toward more focused legislation. One was that administrators of Title I in the Office of Education, many of whom had been recruited because of their commitment to reforms, appreciated legislative backing for what had previously been only administratively determined regulations and guidelines. Another was that members of the congressional committees, and their staffs, had become strongly identified with program objectives; in fact, they were so eager for the program to show positive educational effects that, largely at the initiative of committee staff, they required the Office of Education to identify "exemplary programs" that indicated the kind of Title I programming that was most effective.[13] Still another motivating force was that the National Institute of Education, in its massive study of Title I, had criticized ambiguity of purpose and uncertainty of goals in the administration of the program. In response, Congress decided to give the program more legislative "teeth." Finally, a host of new interest groups that developed expertise in Title I policies reinforced the program's reformist orientation. These groups included the National Advisory Council for the Education of Disadvantaged Children, the National Welfare Rights Organization, the Legal Standards and Education Project of the NAACP, the Lawyers Committee for Civil Rights Under Law, the National Association of Administrators ot Federally-Assisted Education Programs, and the Education Commission of the States.[14]

These new interest groups influenced policy development more through their research and analysis than by the constituency they represented. For example, in the fall of 1969, the NAACP Legal Defense and Educational Fund released a report charging "flagrant violations of the law."[15] In response, the Office of Education formed a task force to examine the issue, and it later substantially increased its administrative staff in charge of securing local compliance. In that same year, a variety of groups coordinated by the Washington Research Project insisted that, inasmuch as research indicated only minimal parental involvement, advisory councils should be mandated. When the Office of Education responded favorably to some of these demands, a spokesman for the National Education Association observed: "USOE has been getting pressure from some groups I've never heard of. I don't know whether they represent a constituency or not."[16] Most important, in 1977 the Lawyers' Committee for Civil Rights Under Law, a Washington-based public interest law firm, took an active interest in ESEA implementation, developing detailed recommendations for strengthening program requirements, preparing manuals that could be used for bringing suits against districts believed to be in violation of Title I statutes, and writing comprehensive analyses of the program's legal framework. In fact, it has been said that "the final 1978 Title I amendments bear a striking resemblance to the draft statute prepared" by a lawyer for this firm.[17]

Policy Implementation

Just as congressional statutes specified the use of Title I funds ever more precisely, so the federal role in the implementation of Title I grew steadily over time. From the very beginning, the Office of Education made clear that the program was intended to provide increased services to children from low-income families. For example, original ground rules provided that, in order to be included in Title I programs, a school had to have a higher concentration of students from low-income families than the school district had as a whole. Still, during the early years, the Office of Education found enforcement of its regulations to be a politically sensitive issue, and its staff was inadequate to handle this assignment. As late as January 1970, there were only three area desk officers who, without any other professional assistance, were responsible for overseeing program implementation in all parts of the United States.[18] Local school districts, not accustomed to furnishing detailed information on local programming to higher administrative agencies, provided only weak substantiation of local compliance. Even when auditors found what appeared to be violations of national guidelines, the Office of Education was reluctant to cut off funds. According to one early (though hardly objective) study:

> The audit reports have brought to light numerous violations of the law and have recommended that millions of dollars be recovered by the Federal government. Yet in only three cases has the Office of Education sought and received restitution of funds illegally spent. . . .[19]

Although the early analyses of program implementation were generally critical, more recent studies have shown higher levels of local compliance. As one longtime analyst of the program argued:

> The common view of Title I administration may be overly pessimistic and unjustified. A more current "end of the decade" view of the federal-state-local partnership could provide a good deal more confidence in the ability of the federal government to influence the operation of categorical programs in local school systems.[20]

Or according to another recent study:

> . . . most states have developed adequate to good procedures for reviewing LEA [local education authorities] applications for Title I funds. These systems have greatly reduced many of the initial problems. . . . At the LEA level, blatant misallocation of funds which clearly violated the intent of Title I have been substantially reduced.[21]

These more optimistic assessments do not mean that all program implementation problems have been resolved. It has been particularly difficult for the Office of Education to ensure that federal funds are used to supplement rather than supplant local resources. During the early 1970s, the top officials in the Office of Education were particularly reluctant to enforce these requirements, even when there was fairly strong evidence that federal funds were used to supplant local funds. One official is quoted as saying, "I've told them [the auditors] I simply won't sustain audit exceptions about supplanting—ever. If that's in there, forget it."[22] The conflicts within the Office of Education on this issue became so great that a National Institute of Education study concluded, "The long-term effects of this dispute may have serious consequences for the program."[23] The study also found that many Office of Education guidelines lacked clarity and that the state's authority to enforce Title I provisions on LEAs was ambiguous.[24]

But for all the ambiguities and difficulties in the administration of the ESEA program, there has been a trend toward more concentrated service delivery. For example, in the early years of the program, the number of students receiving services was considerably larger than the number of "eligible" children; by 1978, program efforts were clearly directed toward pupils from low-income families. As shown in Table 4–2, the ratio of children participating in the program to those eligible for services declined substantially, while expenditures per participating pupil sharply increased. While it may be said that these data indicate that many in need of the services are not receiving them, the more compelling interpretation is that definitions of the population to be served have been narrowed and refined so that, more and more, program participants are educationally disadvantaged students from low-income families.

Table 4–3 illustrates another way to examine the extent to which the program provides services to those who fall within the legislative guideline. According to these findings, the most likely participants in Title I programs were children who were low academic achievers from

Table 4–2 Participation Rates and per Pupil Expenditures under Title I, 1966–78

	Fiscal Year			
	1966	1970	1974	1978
Number of children counted for entitlements[a] (in millions)	5,531	6,952	6,247	9,045
Number of children participating in Title I (in millions)	8,235	7,526	6,100	5,155
Ratio of those participating to those meeting eligibility requirements	1.49	1.08	.98	.57
Title I per pupil (unadjusted dollars) (adjusted dollars)[b]	$117 261	$162 304	$248 363	$379 421

Source: Michael Kirst and Richard Jung, "The Utility of a Longitudinal Approach in Assessing Implementation: A Thirteen Year View of Title I ISEA," *Educational Evaluation and Policy Analysis* 2 (1980).
   a. Figures include only "educationally disadvantaged" children. They do not include handicapped children, juvenile delinquents, children of migrants, or children in agencies for the neglected.
   b. 1979 = 100.

Table 4-3   Percentage of Students Participating in Compensatory Education Programs, by Economic Status and Level of Achievement, 1977

Economic Status	Compensatory Education (CE) Programs			
	Title I/ Title I Plus Other CE	Other CE Only	No CE	Total
Poor				
Low achievement	48.9	10.9	40.2	100.0
Regular achievement	27.4	7.6	65.1	100.1
Not poor				
Low achievement	38.9	15.0	46.1	100.0
Regular achievement	13.1	10.0	76.9	100.0

Source: Vincent J. Breglio, Ronald H. Hinckley, and Richard S. Beal, "Students' Economic and Education Status and Selection for Compensatory Education," Technical Report No. 2, Study of the Sustaining Effects of Compensatory Education on Basic Skills (Santa Monica, Calif.: System Development Corporation, 1978), p. 67.

low-income families. As compared with 48.9 percent of the low achievers from poor families, only 13.1 percent of students who were rated "regular" achievers from families considered "not poor" found their way into the program. Clearly, Title I had found the low-income, low-achieving student population that was intended to be its target. In contrast, compensatory programs paid for by state and local governments did not concentrate their services on low-income or low-achieving students, who were only slightly more likely to be in a state-provided compensatory program than were other pupils. Thus, while nonfederal compensatory programs do exist, Title I alone has directed aid to low academic achievers from low-income families. While some slippage between intention and execution has inevitably occurred—this could be avoided only by extreme federal measures—the federal government may have done so well in making sure that the right students received services that it may have undermined the quality of services provided.

Evaluation of the Educational Impact of Title I

While Title I services have been increasingly directed toward the low-income, educationally disadvantaged pupils for which they were intended, this does not by itself mean that these students have received additional educational benefits. To be sure, it can be argued that, when pupils are taught in smaller classes, have more frequent interaction with adults, or have more adequate materials and supplies, the quality of education has improved. But many people now believe that the proper measure of the effectiveness of an educational program is improvement in the test scores of students participating in the program. Congress thus mandated in 1965, and even more clearly in subsequent amendments to the law, that extensive evaluations of Title I programs should be undertaken. Although critics have questioned the methodological validity of these evaluations, it is of interest that almost none of the major studies found more than the most modest educational impact.

Evaluation was required by the original ESEA legislation largely at Robert Kennedy's insistence: "I have seen enough school districts where there has been a lack of imagination, lack of initiative, and lack of interest in the problems of the deprived children. . . . My feeling is that even if we put money into those school districts, then it will be wasted."[25] Other policymakers were more optimistic about overall program effectiveness but still believed that evaluations could help identify appropriate strategies for providing compensatory education services.

Two different kinds of evaluations have been conducted. First, local school officials have been required to conduct their own evaluations, which they must then report to state and federal officials. In the early years of the program, most of these evaluations were either informal assessments or performed at such a low level of technical competence that their findings had little value. In the words of an analyst of these early evaluations, "Most Title I project reports continue to resemble educational travel brochures, with extensive anecdotes and little objective data to support claims of 'success.' "[26]

Congress became concerned about the quality of these early studies and in 1974 directed the commissioner of education to provide "models" for evaluations, which were to include "uniform procedures and criteria" to be utilized by state and local agencies.[27] In response to this directive, the Office of Education asked the Research Management Corporation (RMC) to propose a number of scientifically acceptable models. The following three models were accepted: (1) Tests were to be administered to students before and after they participated in the program. Their rates of improvement would be compared with the scores obtained from state and national norms for all pupils at that grade level. (2) The test group would be compared with a control group of students not participating in the program. Ideally, the test and control groups of students would be selected at random from a single population. (3) Comparisons between the test and control groups would be made by means of a "special regression design." Any relevant characteristics that distinguished the test from the control groups would be entered into the regression model as control variables.

There are problems associated with each model. Students are seldom, if ever, randomly assigned to Title I programs, as required by the second model; making such assignments would run counter to the spirit of ESEA legislation. Regression models, such as the third model, are subject to specification error if a significant characteristic is not included in the regression. Since no theory as to which characteristics are relevant has ever gained general acceptance in the social science community, any regression equation is open to the criticism that it has misspecified observed relationships. But the model with the greatest validity problems is the first one, the very model most frequently used by local school districts because it is the easiest to administer. This model yields correct results only if the test group can be understood as a random sample from the state or national population against which it is being compared. Since children in need of compensatory education are by definition not drawn randomly, the validity of evaluations based on this model is open to strong criticism.

Local officials are quite aware of these and other problems with their own evaluations. According to Jane David, who conducted a nationwide study of the local uses to which evaluations have been put, "There is little doubt that the primary function the evaluations serve is to meet the state and Federal reporting requirements of Title I."[28] She found little evidence that such evaluations were used to give feedback to parents, to make program decisions, or even to determine whether or not the program was effective. She quoted one teacher who observed that "The main purpose the test scores serve is to support your own views,"[29] and a school superintendent who stated straightforwardly that "I want information to justify expansion of the program. I'm not interested in information showing students are behind national norms."[30]

A comparison of two major analyses of state and local evaluations of Title I programs illustrates some of the difficulties of using these data. The first study, carried out by RMC in 1974–75, reached generally pessimistic conclusions about the effectiveness of Title I. While the study observed that "children were making a month gain for each month of instruction," various biases and inconsistencies in the data led the authors to conclude that "actual [student] gains were smaller than those reported."[31] In other words, students in these programs were not even making progress at a normal rate. The second study, carried out shortly thereafter by the Stanford Research Institute (SRI), reached far more optimistic conclusions, even though the data sets being analyzed in the two studies overlapped substantially. SRI found that, on the average, students were making about 1.1 month's gain in performance for every month of instruction they were receiving, a finding not substantially different from RMC's finding. But SRI believed that these pupils would have attained only a 0.7 month's gain in performance for every month of instruction had there been no Title I program. As a result, the program achieved more than a "50% increase in the achievement rate" of disadvantaged students.[32] Thus, depending on the way the data are interpreted, Title I students can be said to be making either no greater progress than would have been made otherwise or to be learning at a rate 50 percent greater than what might have been expected. Clearly, one difficulty with the state and local evaluation data is that they leave the relevant point of comparison to the researcher's imagination.

Because of these and other difficulties with the state and local evaluations, the Office of Education has also attempted to assess the quality of Title I programs through a second kind of evaluation—nationally administered tests given by independent testing agencies. While the methodology of these studies has also been criticized, the studies do have the advantage of being administered by people with greater technical expertise and no obvious program bias. On the other hand, these independent national evaluations often hide significant variations in program design and implementation, thus making it difficult to ascertain what kinds of Title I programs are the most effective.

The first major independent evaluation whose results can be treated with some credence was undertaken by the Educational Testing Service (ETS) in 1972–73. Before-and-after tests were administered to a sample of more than 40,000 students in compensatory education programs as well as to a control group of students in noncompensatory education programs. Data were analyzed by a wide variety of techniques, including a complex regression analysis. The study found no substantial differences on a wide range of tests between the performances of pupils in Title I programs and those of pupils in the control group non-Title I programs. The report's summary stated that "all of the analyses supported the assertion that compensatory students tend not to fall further behind noncompensatory students during the academic year."[33] In other words, Title I resources at least did the children no harm.

While the quality of the ETS 1972–73 data collection and analysis far surpassed that of any prior Title I study undertaken on a national scale, a number of criticisms nonetheless cast doubt on the validity of its findings. Apart from several technical deficiencies, it seems that

ETS did not eliminate from its analysis those pupils who took only the before-test or only the after-test.[34] As a result, comparisons were being made between the before-and-after performances of somewhat different groups of pupils. Had these cases been removed from the analysis, it is conceivable that different results might have been obtained.

More recently, a second major independent study of Title I has been conducted by Systems Development Corporation (SDC). In contrast to the ETS study, SDC reports that compensatory education "has had consistently positive effects on achievement growth," effects that, on average, amount to approximately a 1.1 months' gain for every month of instruction.[35] Yet even this comparatively optimistic assessment concludes that the "beneficial effects of compensatory education, while detectable, are not large."[36]

When considered as a whole, Title I evaluations give the general impression that the effects of these compensatory education programs vary so widely from place to place that, on the average, they do not have an impact substantial enough to be measured easily. Although the methodology of all of the studies is open to criticism, the findings are remarkably consistent in detecting no more than small benefits nationwide. In this respect, the studies are also consistent with the findings of the National Assessment of Educational Progress presented in chapter 2, which found only slight changes in educational performance at the elementary-school level (where Title I monies have been concentrated), but slightly better trends for children from less well educated families, for children from rural areas, and for children who are members of a racial minority. It is impossible to ascertain how much of this modest improvement for disadvantaged groups, as compared with other pupils, is due to Title I. It may be that the positive effects of compensatory education programs for children from low-income families, and especially for racial minorities, lie not so much in the specific benefits of any single set of services as in the general benefits created by the federal government's commitment to equal educational opportunity.

Problems in the Implementation of Title I

Administrative Costs

While the precise educational impact of Title I cannot be easily specified, local officials have for some time been well aware of the program's administrative costs. In order to show compliance with Title I regulations, LEAs must demonstrate, among other things, that their programs are concentrated in schools where educational deficiencies are the greatest, that Title I schools are being funded from local sources at a level comparable with other schools in the district, that federal funds have not merely "supplanted" local funds that would otherwise have been spent, that local programs are developed and implemented on the "advice" of parent councils, and that the children receiving the services in Title I schools are, in fact, the educationally disadvantaged. No wonder a Chicago school official, when testifying before Congress in 1973, complained that "an annual gathering of this type of data in the large urban school system is an expensive, complex, and time-consuming process."[37] His testimony was corroborated by the Milwaukee school superintendent who objected to "serious impediments" in administering Title I programs, such as uncertain timing and levels of funding, problems in assessing whether resources in Title I schools are comparable with those in other schools, and the difficulties of involving parent advisory councils.[38]

The administrative costs of Title I and other federal programs do seem substantial. According to one study, each new dollar of federal funds creates nine times the increase in administrative personnel that each new dollar of local money creates.[39] While it is difficult to know the extent to which the findings from this study can be generalized, it is worth noting that administrative costs, which, for more than three decades, had hovered between 4.3 and 4.7 percent of the total current expenditures in education, increased to 5.3 percent between 1970 and 1978; they dropped in 1979–80, but only to 4.9 percent (see Table 4–4). Apparently, in this short period of time, increased centralization of school finance at state and national levels, together with the growing formalization of many school procedures (induced by numerous court decisions designed to protect student and parental rights) have raised overall administrative costs. While the percentage increases are not massive, the 0.7 percent increment from 1970–78 amounted to additional spending of more than $500 million in 1977–78 alone.

Pull-out Programs

Higher administrative costs may be justified if they are necessary to ensure that effective educational services are reaching disadvantaged children. But in the case of Title I, at least some of the educational innovations inspired by federal regulation seem counterproductive. One in particular is so widespread and central to Title I programming that it deserves detailed attention: the pull-out program. This program

Table 4–4   Breakdown of Current Expenditures in Elementary and Secondary Public Schools,
1929–80

	1929–30	1939–40	1949–50	1959–60	1969–70	1977–78	1979–80
Current expenditures, public elementary and secondary schools (in billions)	$1.8	$1.9	$4.7	$12.3	$34.2	$73.1	$87.0
Percent of current expenditures for:							
Administration	4.3%	4.7%	4.7%	4.3%	4.6%	5.3%	4.9%
Instruction	71.5	72.3	66.4	67.5	68.0	61.6	61.2
Plant operation and maintenance	16.0	13.8	13.7	12.2	10.2	11.0	11.2
Fixed charges	2.7	2.5	5.6	7.3	9.5	12.7	13.6
Other services[a]	5.5	6.6	9.6	8.4	7.5	9.3	9.1
Total percent	100.0	99.9	100.0	99.7	99.8	99.9	100.0

Source: Department of Education, National Center for Education Statistics, *Digest of Education Statistics* (Washington, D.C.:
Government Printing Office, 1980, 1982 eds.).
Note: Total percentages do not always equal 100 because of rounding.
a. Other services include attendance, health, transportation, food services, and pupil activities paid for out of tax revenues.
Prior to 1950-60, it also includes community services.

removes elementary-school pupils from their regular classrooms to give them concentrated training in reading or arithmetic under the tutelage of special teachers, either in small classes or on a one-to-one basis.

The pull-out program is constitutionally dubious, educationally questionable, insupportable by the evidence from most evaluations, and never explicitly required by either Congress or the Office of Education. Yet while nothing in Title I or Office of Education guidelines specifically mandates pull-out programs, many school officials believe them to be obligatory, and more than half the Title I compensatory education programs take this form. Further, federal regulations and auditing practices clearly encourage their use. If any changes in federal policy are to be undertaken, attention should first be given to the pull-out program.

Pull-out programs are attractive because they easily fulfill the bureaucratic requirements attached to Title I funding. For example, federal regulations require that funding recipients be educationally disadvantaged. Since pull-out programs can be focused squarely on eligible pupils, it can be clearly established, for purposes of a federal audit, that the targeted pupils within a school are receiving the supplementary services. Second, it is not difficult to prove that pull-out programs are supplemental to, not supplantive of, locally financed education. If special teachers and aides are hired exclusively for Title I purposes, and if, when not "pulled out," students participate in regular classrooms, then the supplemental quality of the service can be indubitably established. Third, pull-out programs can be easily discontinued if federal funds are cut or if a school loses its Title I eligibility. Fourth, Title I intrudes as little as possible on the traditional autonomy of the classroom teacher. The teacher may find the class disrupted periodically as pupils leave and return to class, but for the most part has the advantage of working with a smaller class (and probably without some of the more demanding pupils). Fifth, the federal government's attempt to allocate resources not just to states, districts, and schools, but to classrooms within schools, and students within classrooms, encourages local administrators to favor pull-out programs.

The pull-out programs make bureaucratic sense, but hardly seem compelled by pedagogical theory. While a child may benefit from small classes and tutorials, there are definite costs to being pulled out of the regular class. The child may lose continuity with the regular school lesson, may spend considerable time coming and going from one teacher to another, and may suffer the stigma of requiring special treatment. Much of the success of the program depends on the relative merits of the regular and the special teachers. Since the regular teacher has the more stable position, it is possible that more often than not the child is leaving the more qualified, more experienced teacher for one less competent.

Evaluations of Title I have seldom found pull-out programs to be effective. In one study, William W. Cooley and Gaea Leinhardt found pull-out programs considerably less efficacious than programs integrated into the regular classroom experience.[40] The SDC study, moreover, found that "evidence for positive effects of special instruction on achievement growth is sparse."[41] G. V. Glass and M. L. Smith, after analyzing the evidence on pull-out programs, "concluded that they are not educationally sound." They found no evidence "that the practice facilitated achievement, and ample evidence that the unintended negative side effects of "labelling pupils are large and worrisome."[42]

Further, since pull-out programs select certain students for learning in a separate environment, they are legally suspect. Their possible disproportionate use in racially mixed schools makes them doubly so.[43]

Thus, the intense federal effort to ensure that Title I services be geared to low-income, educationally disadvantaged pupils has been carried to such an extreme as to constrain educational practice along lines that are dubious at best. While the federal government would be ill-advised to outlaw pull-out programs if local officials prefer them, such practices should not be actively, however subtly, encouraged. Fortunately, in the past few years there seems to have been a marked reduction in the use of this pull-out concept.

Conclusions

Compensatory education under Title I illustrates both the promises and pitfalls of federal involvement in elementary and secondary education. On the one hand, the program seeks to assist those who have not been well served by state and local governments: the poor, racial minorities, and the educationally disadvantaged, who all lack political influence and economic leverage.

If local schools do not well serve the productive, middle-class segment of the community, these groups will seek better schools elsewhere, and the cost in terms of taxes, property values, and quality of business and commercial life can be high. But if local schools do not well serve the children of poor minorities, the economic loss to the community is less severe; their families may leave the area, but this hardly disturbs local property values. In fact, it may be especially costly for the community to provide high-quality schools for the poor, since good schools only attract more poor people to the area. Thus, it has become appropriate for the federal government to take a special interest in the educational needs of low-income groups.

On the other hand, the program exposes the limits of a policy that is too specific about the way in which education should be conducted. Over time, Title I laws and regulations have become increasingly rigorous and complex. Given initial LEA resistance to using the monies exclusively for low-income children, such policies have had a certain logic. But the federal government may have gone too far in seeking detailed compliance with its numerous regulations. If the intergovernmental partnership in education is to succeed, the federal government must recognize that the processes of education are too complex to be easily manipulated by central policymakers. When attempts to achieve compliance penetrate to the classroom, they intervene in situations that can be satisfactorily worked out only by those closest at hand. The federal government needs to learn ways to fulfill its educational objective—providing equal educational opportunity—without impeding any educational opportunities, equal or not.

Drawing on experience from Title I pull-out programs, the following proposal might be made: federal policy should be restricted to assuring fair, equitable allocation of tangible resources; how these resources are to be used should be left to the principals and teachers of local schools. A federal policy that touches the classroom has penetrated beyond the point where it can have positive consequences.

Effective school administration and good teaching remain art forms that do not benefit from precise stipulation by central authorities. Not only do we not know what makes for good teaching, it would probably be impossible to prescribe the activity if we did. Teaching and learning are most satisfying when the participants have a sense of autonomy. While teachers can be encouraged by their co-workers and inspired by an enthusiastic principal, it is not possible to mandate high-quality teaching from afar.

5
THE EXPANSION:
NEW APPROACHES TO EQUALITY

Once the Elementary and Secondary Education Act (ESEA) had identified a distinct federal purpose in education—the provision of equal educational opportunity—it was used to justify numerous requests for congressional action. Those for whom English was a second language, the physically and mentally handicapped, and those receiving racially segregated schooling all appealed to Washington for funds to allow them equal access to education. Congress responded by authorizing the Office of Education to develop programs in these three areas. In each case, local school districts were asked not just to do more than they had been doing, but to do things differently. Even more than had been the case with ESEA, the expectation was that federal assistance would be accompanied by reform.

The fact that all three of these programs were in response to prior judicially induced changes in the educational system shows how far federal education policy had moved toward promoting equal opportunity. Bilingual education was given impetus by the Supreme Court's 1974 *Lau v. Nichols* decision, which held that the Civil Rights Act required local school districts to take into account the special needs of those whose native tongue was not English. Washington was awakened to the needs of the handicapped when two lower court decisions, which stated that retarded children could not be excluded from public schools, were never appealed. The Emergency School Aid Act was prompted by a series of court decisions in the late 1960s that gave sharper teeth to the Supreme Court's 1954 *Brown v. Board of Education* decision. Clearly, the courts were expecting new things of schools. Both the petitioning groups and, to some extent, school officials themselves turned to Congress and the Office of Education for the direction and funding to meet these expectations.

107

These three new programs, like the compensatory education program that preceded them, were directed toward solving problems that had not been adequately addressed by most local school districts. Consequently, the programs gained vigorous support in Washington from specialized interests and a related cadre of professionals, from which an administrative staff deeply committed to program objectives was recruited. This intense commitment, however, also encouraged a tendency toward overadministration of program policy. Local school districts were regarded as suspect and in need of reform. To ensure program objectives, federal officials often specified exact procedures in areas and on topics where the "one best way" was not easily determined. And problems were created when "exacting" requirements had to be applied to the variety of local school districts in the United States. Evaluations of local progress were conducted at times and in ways that were often utterly inappropriate. As laudable as federal motives might have been, the consequences were more varied and less satisfying than many had hoped.

Confusion was especially apparent in the attempt to define equal educational opportunity. While the concept was used to legitimate nearly all the claims for federal funding that were being made, each of the interest groups making these claims understood the meaning of equal opportunity in a somewhat different way. For some, equality required identical treatment. Supporters of federal funding to desegregate public schools, for example, believed that only by integrating students could the scars of racial differentiation be healed. Or in the case of handicapped children, advocates urged that the law provide the "least restrictive environment" possible. For others, equality required distinctive treatment. Just as many compensatory programs under Title I pulled educationally disadvantaged children out of the regular classroom, so others supported bilingual programs that would provide separate instructional settings for those children whose native tongue was not English.

Each of these federal programs, with its own definition of equal opportunity, required its own set of federal guidelines. Thus, the Office of Education worked out rules appropriate for each piece of legislation. But local officials became increasingly distressed not only at the extent and complexity of the requirements they faced, but also at the inconsistencies in federal expectations. What was required in one program was outlawed in another. Resources necessary for the success of one policy placed other federal programs in jeopardy. At the national level, policymakers tried to resolve these difficulties by making exceptions, waiving requirements, and reaching compromises. But these attempts at integrating federal education policy only further contributed to the overall complexity of a highly fragmented system of categorical grants.

On all sides, new demands for coordination and simplification emerged.

The complexity of the present picture will best be understood if each of these new federal attempts to provide equal educational opportunity—bilingual education, education for the handicapped, and aid for school desegregation—is examined separately. Each case will illustrate how federal involvement grew out of dissatisfaction with local practices, how the emphasis on reform led to regulation and control by federal officials, and how regulatory policy complicated the lives of educational practitioners at the local level.

Bilingual Education

Bilingual education most graphically illustrates the pattern just described. Federal policy was in direct response to new political pressures emerging from a previously quiescent Spanish-speaking community. Although the demands for bilingual education struck a responsive chord in a few cities, on a national scale the policy was not popular. The office formed to implement federal policy on bilingual education was received without enthusiasm by many local school districts, and the consequent efforts by the Office of Education to define the structure and content of bilingual instruction entered administrative and educational areas better left to local judgment and discretion.

Demands for bilingual education were an early by-product of a rising political consciousness among Puerto Ricans, Mexican-Americans, and other ethnic groups awakened by the civil-rights movement. Language had been an issue in American education in the nineteenth century, when Germans and other European immigrant groups sought instruction in their native tongue. But the closeness of the Anglo-American alliance through two world wars had dampened political support for education in other languages. By the 1960s, twenty-eight states "had laws requiring English as the language of instruction in the public schools. In seven states, including Texas, a teacher could be subject to criminal penalties or lose his teaching license if he taught bilingually."[1]

Policy Development

While a variety of locally sponsored bilingual programs were undertaken in scattered districts in Florida and the Southwest, from the very beginning, the political drive for bilingual education, as for much of the civil-rights movement, focused on Washington. Its initial sponsor was Senator Ralph Yarborough, the Texas liberal Democrat who had long been popular among Spanish-Americans. Organizations such as the Texas GI Forum, the Political Association of Spanish-speaking Organizations in Texas, and additional groups from Texas to California supported Yarborough and other liberal Democrats—such as Senator Edward Kennedy and Representative James Scheuer, who represented a Puerto Rican constituency in New York City—in their efforts to secure federal funding for bilingual education. These congressmen successfully added a seventh title to ESEA in 1968, which authorized a limited number of demonstration projects in bilingual education. In 1969, the first year of Title VII funding, seventy-nine projects serving 26,500 students were established at a cost of $7.5 million.

Despite its modest beginnings, the bilingual education program grew rapidly. As shown in Table 3–1, it expanded in size to $26 million in 1972, to $79.5 million in 1976, and to $156.4 million by 1980. The fiscal magnitude of the program is only one measure of its growth; the program also developed an increasingly solid legislative footing. In 1972, funds were earmarked for bilingual education programs as part of the Emergency School Aid Act because these programs were considered "one of the tools utilized in carrying out a desegregation plan involving national origin students."[2] In 1974, Title VII of ESEA was amended in order to expand its scope and significance. Instead of simply authorizing a limited number of projects, the 1974 act, while formally maintaining the program on only a "demonstration" basis, elevated the "branch" of bilingual education to the status of an "office" within the larger Office of Education and, in the words of Representative Patricia Schroeder (D.-Colorado), established:

> . . . a bilingual vocational training program, an expanded program for the training of bilingual education teachers and other educational personnel; an in-depth research program by the National Institute of Education to develop better teaching methods and materials; a national survey of the number of children and adults with limited English-speaking ability and the extent to which they are being served by Federal, State and local programs; and a strengthened independent National Advisory Council on Bilingual Education.[3]

In addition, the legislation authorized graduate fellowships in bilingual education and the establishment of centers for the development, assessment, and dissemination of bilingual curricular materials. Title VII of ESEA was amended once again in 1978, but the changes were relatively minor. Parent participation was encouraged, evaluations were required, and the law identified the group to be served as "not proficient in English," rather than "non-English speaking."

Once bilingual education was deemed appropriate for pupils from homes where English was not spoken proficiently, the program expanded rapidly; still, it was unable to meet student needs. Although by 1978, over 300,000 pupils were participating in 567 different bilingual programs,[4] estimates of the number of school-age children in need of bilingual education exceeded six million (see Table 5-1). Congress's reluctance to declare its bilingual education policy as anything more than a series of "demonstration" projects was largely due, it would seem, to the substantial fiscal commitment that would be required if all children eligible for the program were to receive federal assistance.

The needs of schoolchildren for bilingual education were not the main force driving program expansion. While the number of Asian and Spanish-speaking children had increased substantially throughout the 1970s (see Table 2-2), non-English-speaking Americans had been attending the nation's public schools for decades. It was various political pressures, more than demographic changes, that pushed the pro-

Table 5-1 Household Languages of the Population, Four Years Old and Over, by Age, 1975

Language Spoken in Household	4 to 5 Years Old	6 to 18 Years Old	Total Population
	(in thousands)		
English only	6,125	43,335	167,665
Total other language as usual or second language	928	6,738	25,347[c]
Spanish	524	3,279	9,904
French	a	623	2,259
German	60	527	2,269
Greek	a	124	488
Italian	68	599	2,836
Portuguese	a	87	349
Chinese	a	120	534
Filipino	a	133	377
Japanese	a	129	524
Korean	a	73	246
Other	133	1,044	5,559
Not reported	a	680	3,786
Grand total[b]	6,910	50,753	196,796

Source: Department of Education, National Center for Education Statistics, *The Condition of Education* (Washington, D.C.: Government Printing Office, 1977), p. 149.
    a. Fewer than an estimated 50,000 persons.
    b. Grand total includes those nationalities of fewer than 50,000.
    c. Detail may not add to totals due to rounding.

gram forward. Not only did the program receive strong support from minority educators, including staff members of the National Education Association, but it had widespread political support among community organizations in the Mexican-American and Puerto Rican communities. Groups such as the National Congress of Hispanic American Citizens, the Puerto Rican Forum, the Puerto Rican Association for National Affairs, the ASPIRA of America all testified on behalf of the program and made bilingual education central to their endorsement of candidates for political office.

While other ethnic groups supported federal bilingual education policy, the popularity of the program in the Spanish-speaking community has been primarily responsible for its expansion. Bilingual education has become almost as symbolically significant to this ethnic minority as school integration has been to blacks. While black leaders have believed that only through integration could their identity as equal members of the American political community be affirmed, Spanish-speaking leaders, much less interested in integration per se, have emphasized the need for public affirmation of the worthiness of their language and culture.

Unlike many of the earlier immigrant groups, those from Mexico, Puerto Rico, other islands in the Caribbean, and other parts of Latin America have maintained continuous contacts with their homeland, aided by geographic proximity and improved international transportation. Life in the United States' "barrios" continues to beat to a Latin rhythm, and in 1976, over 41 percent of all families from Spanish-speaking countries still spoke Spanish in their homes.[5] The fact that schools refused to accept Spanish as a legitimate means of communication was viewed as an insult to these homes and neighborhoods. In order for community leaders from these areas to gain political acceptance for their constituents, they have therefore attempted to obtain validation of their language by the public schools.

While some school officials have not been entirely responsive to these concerns, elected public officials, always sensitive to ethnic issues, have eagerly embraced the bilingual cause. Not surprisingly, its chief supporters are members of Congress from states and districts with sizable Spanish-speaking constituencies. In addition to backing from Yarborough and Scheuer, bilingual education received steady support from Senators Alan Cranston (D.–California) and Joseph Montoya (D.–New Mexico) and Representatives Shirley Chisholm (D.–New York), Alphonzo Bell (R.–California), and Edward R. Roybal (D.–California). Under the general umbrella provided by these public figures, congressional staff members, working in cooperation with interest group leaders and officials within the Office of Education, have pressed the bilingual cause. As is the case with most policies of great concern to a few congressmen and of marginal concern to the majority, their efforts in committees and subcommittees have yielded substantial dividends in legislative support. The best evidence of this is the fiscal support the program has received; in almost every year since bilingual education was authorized, congressional appropriations have exceeded presidential requests (see Table 5-2).

Table 5-2 Federal Funding for Bilingual Education,[a] 1969–84 (in current dollars)

Fiscal Year	Budget Requested by the Administration (in thousands)	Amount Appropriated by the Congress (in thousands)
1969	$ 5,000	$ 7,000
1970	10,000	21,250
1971	10,000	25,000
1972	25,000	35,000
1973	41,130	45,000
1974	35,000	58,350[b]
1975	35,000	85,000
1976	70,000	94,970
1977	90,000	115,000
1978	90,000	135,000
1979	150,000	173,600
1980	173,600	118,963
1982	c	138,057
1983	94,534	138,057
1984	94,534	—

Sources: The Budget, Senate Committee on Appropriations Reports and Related Conference Reports; Susan Gilbert Schneider, *Revolution, Reaction or Reform* (New York: Las Americas, 1977); *Education Week*, January 26, 1983.
   a. Under the authority of Title VII of ESEA.
   b. $9.87 million of this appropriation was impounded and then released on December 19, 1973. Of the amount released, $170,000 was to be expended in fiscal 1974 and $9.7 million in fiscal 1975.
   c. Reagan administration proposed no funds.

National political leaders, including presidents and their administrative aides, have been much more ambivalent about bilingual education. In general, a presidential candidate, or an incumbent president seeking reelection, is more supportive than a president attempting to balance the federal budget during the annual appropriations process. Aspiring presidential candidates Walter Mondale and Edward Kennedy, for example, were among the program's strongest advocates. Presidents were much less supportive. The Johnson administration urged that, instead of adding a new program, bilingual education be financed under Title I; the Nixon administration wished to include Title VII in its consolidation of educational programs, thereby eliminating the program's independent legislative basis as well as its own administrative staff; and Gerald Ford reluctantly signed the 1974 amendments into law, largely to calm the bitter confrontations that Watergate had provoked between the executive and legislative branches. President Reagan has systematically sought to diminish the size and significance of the program by cutting its fiscal base and by weakening bilingual regulations. By comparison, the Carter administration proved a much better friend of bilingual education. Carter appointed an activist program director and nominated Shirley Hufstedler, a federal judge who had indicated her favorable assessment of bilingual education in a lower court decision, as secretary of education. In fact, Secretary Hufstedler prepared a complex set of regulations that had reached the point of promulgation before they were withdrawn during the first weeks of the Reagan administration.

National political leaders must choose between the urgent demands of minorities and the broader, less intense feelings of the population as a whole. While little enthusiasm for—and perhaps a good deal of opposition to—bilingual education can be found among the English-speaking majority, bilingual education has been of great concern to many Latinos. In a political system where majorities are often built out of ethnic coalitions, candidates for high office have every incentive to give careful consideration to such programs as bilingual education. Democratic leaders, traditionally the most assiduous devotees of ethnic politics, have generally been the most responsive. But Republican leaders, who wish to attain and hold the support of Spanish-speaking voters in order to help offset overwhelmingly Democratic majorities among blacks, have seldom openly attacked bilingual education. For example, the Reagan administration, though critical of strong regulations enforcing bilingualism and despite its overall preference to bundle most existing categorical programs into block grants, agreed to maintain a separate categorical program for bilingual education.

While political bases of support have been necessary to sustain the bilingual education program throughout the 1970s, its biggest boost came in the form of a Supreme Court decision (*Lau v. Nichols,* 1974) that required local school districts to take linguistic heritage into account. In interpreting the Civil Rights Act of 1964, the Court did not specify what form of treatment was required for students for whom English was not the first language, but did state that the simple provision of the same facilities, textbooks, teachers, and curriculum as provided to English-speaking students insufficiently responded to the needs of those not proficient in the language.

Policy Implementation

While court decisions and political pressures facilitated the establishment of a federal bilingual education policy, they had less effect on acceptance of the program at the local level. The enthusiasm that Spanish-speaking leaders and certain members of Congress demonstrated for bilingual education was not generally shared by local school boards or their top administrative staffs; in fact, there was resistance in many localities. Consequently, the Office of Education developed an increasing array of rules designed to ensure compliance. Since funding for bilingual education programs was only modest, local officials particularly resented these guidelines.

Bilingual education, it must be remembered, has never been more than a "demonstration" program, and Congress has yet to agree that it has a responsibility to fund special services for all children who lack English language proficiency. Thus, the program, even though it has expanded greatly, is small in comparison with Title I, vocational education, or impact aid. Moreover, as a demonstration program, Title VII provides no set formula for distributing funds among the states and localities; grants are awarded to school districts in response to applications for assistance.

In the final year of the Carter administration, the Office of Civil Rights in the Department of Education proposed bilingual education requirements for all districts with a substantial number of non-English-speaking minorities. In a formal sense, these regulations had nothing to do with Title VII per se. Instead, they represented the Department of Education's view of the kinds of programs local school districts must have to be considered in compliance with the Civil Rights Act of 1964 as interpreted by the Supreme Court in *Lau v. Nichols.* The Department of Education expected every school district with a non-English-speaking minority to demonstrate compliance with these regulations, if it was to receive any federal aid at all. Although never formally adopted, these regulations are of interest because they emerged out of the department's experience with the bilingual education demonstration program and because they were a formalization of department thinking on bilingual education.

While many of the provisions of the proposed regulations involved complex matters and controversial decisions, the choice between "transitional" and "maintenance" bilingual education programs proved especially difficult to resolve. "Transitional" programs use the student's primary, or non-English, language to teach English proficiency as quickly as possible; "maintenance" programs preserve the student's cultural heritage and maintain the nation's language resources by educating pupils in the language they know best. Many of the most ardent advocates of bilingual education prefer the "maintenance" program concept, but Congress and the Department of Education have in recent years found such programs politically unacceptable and have required local authorities to provide "transitional" services only (although the present law also requires that programs show respect for the child's home culture).

In practice, transitional and maintenance programs are not easily distinguishable, and it has proven difficult for the Department of Education to ensure that only "transitional" programs are funded. In response to criticisms that funds were being used to support maintenance programs, the department has required that 30 percent of all pupils participating in bilingual education programs be English-speaking and that non-English-speaking students leave the program once they have achieved a certain level of proficiency in the English language.

Both provisions have created problems for local school administrators. As desirable as it may be to have English-speaking playmates for non-English-speaking students, the rationale for requiring English-speaking children to take classes conducted in a foreign language is far from clear. Further, the rule that students must leave the program if they are becoming proficient in English cuts two ways; it hardly seems sensible to move a child out of an environment in which learning is taking place. One well-conceived and popular bilingual education program, offered in San Diego, has courses given only in the Spanish language, even though half of the students enrolled speak English. After several years in the program, children acquire a high level of proficiency in both languages, and many English-speaking parents are eager to send their children to this magnet school that attracts students from across the city. Yet if Department of Education guidelines were inflexibly applied, Spanish-speaking children would have to leave this high-quality program as their English-language skills developed.

Basically, the problem is not whether a transitional or maintenance approach should be followed. Under certain circumstances, either one may be entirely appropriate. The problem is that the conditions under which bilingual education is being provided are so diverse that it is beyond the capacity of the federal government to lay down such specific guidelines. Whatever biases local principals and teachers may have, at least they know the specific circumstances in which they provide education. It is highly unlikely that national policymakers can correctly specify the percentage of English-speaking and non-English-speaking children necessary to give a curriculum a "transitional" quality; their efforts to allocate resources within schools and to shape the student composition of specific programs are as likely to be misguided as they are to be suitable. The Department of Education administrators are under political pressure to preserve the bilingual education program and to defend it against criticism that it is building a two-language society. But local school officials are correct when they say that our knowledge of bilingual education is not sufficiently advanced to allow for central determination of program design.

Program Evaluation

The first national independent evaluation of bilingual education was conducted by American Institutes for Research (AIR). Thirty-eight Spanish/English bilingual projects in "either their fourth or fifth year of funding as of fall 1975" were evaluated. At least two classes from grades two through six were tested in English at both the beginning and end of the school year. Local Title VII personnel were asked to nominate comparable classes not participating in the program to serve as control groups. On the basis of this research, the AIR study concluded that "in terms of one of the major goals of the ESEA Title VII legislation—that of having students of limited English-speaking ability achieve competency in the English language—the projects which have been operating four to five years have not been generally effective."[6] The study found that students in the bilingual education program did better than students in the control groups on math tests, but worse on reading and vocabulary.

The study, released shortly before the opening of the reauthorization hearings for Title VII in 1978, may have dampened congressional enthusiasm for bilingual education; it certainly prompted demands for further studies and evaluations. But the impact of the study was softened by the strong criticism it received from social scientists and bilingual education advocates, who were especially disturbed by the method of control groups selection. Not only did nearly half the local

Title VII administrators fail to make any selection at all, but it is doubtful that the remainder had the necessary information to identify accurately a matched group (which ideally should be a random sample from the same population as the experimental group). It was discovered that students in the so-called control groups were considerably more likely to use English than any other language. Thus, it is hardly surprising that these so-called comparison students should have gained more in English reading comprehension over the course of the year.

Critics also noted that many of the so-called bilingual programs did not have the staff or materials to qualify as truly bilingual. One of the reasons why it is so difficult to evaluate bilingual programs is that they are constantly developing new techniques, new curricular materials, and new training for teachers. Any evaluation is likely to be describing programs that will shortly be out of date. The effectiveness of bilingual education will continue to be debated, but that debate is unlikely to be readily informed by formal evaluations of program effectiveness.

Bilingual education advocates claim that bilingual programs increase the likelihood that secondary students will remain in school. By reducing the distance between the culture of home and school, bilingual instruction achieves greater acceptance among Hispanic youth. Preliminary findings from the National Opinion Research Center study of high-school sophomores and seniors, conducted in May 1980, tend to confirm these claims. According to this study, "In the presence of a bilingual program, the excess of the Hispanic dropout rate [the difference between Hispanics and other students] is cut in half"; in the absence of such programs, "dropout among Hispanic students may actually run as high as 20 percent or more." The study also notes that "Hispanic faculty teaching at the school . . . also seem to make a difference in reducing dropout."[7] Even if bilingual education programs do nothing more than increase the number of Spanish-speaking school staff members, that may be sufficient reason for many Hispanics to support these programs.

Summary

Bilingual education is very much a political issue. As Noel Epstein observed, "There is no question that bilingual-bicultural policy has been governed in large measure by the quest of discriminated-against minority groups, and particularly Hispanic Americans, for more power, prestige and jobs."[8] Federal (and, in some places, state) responsiveness to these demands testifies to the growing political significance of the Hispanic community. That the bilingual education program evolved largely in response to national directives also indicates the extent to which the federal government has become the most sensitive outlet for minority demands and the main vehicle for expressing the nation's commitment to equal educational opportunity.

Yet the implementation of bilingual programs reveals the awkwardness with which the federal government responds to complex educational issues. Finding the balance between transitional and maintenance programs, or favoring one over the other, involves creating arbitrary quotas for entry into and exit from bilingual education programs. National policymakers begin regulating the traffic in and out of the classroom. As complex as the issues have become, the federal government is best advised to avoid making choices between one kind of bilingual education program and another, leaving to local officials the decisions that make sense for their own communities. As Gary Orfield observed:

> Reading the existing research on bilingualism makes one point very clear—we do not know enough to make any confident global prescriptions. . . . Probably we eventually will discover that there is no single best answer and that bilingualism works well only for certain purposes in certain settings.[9]

Education for the Handicapped

The concept of equal opportunity opened up new vistas for non-English-speaking minorities, but innovations to benefit non-English-speaking members of the community pale in comparison with new provisions for the handicapped. While the most dramatic changes occurred in the areas of employment and public accommodation, education programs for the handicapped were also greatly expanded during the 1970s. As in the case of bilingual education, program development was urged on by well-organized interest groups and key congressional supporters in the face of considerable resistance from the executive branch. Judicial decisions that legitimated the claims of the handicapped also proved critical.

The legislation incorporating these political developments—the Education for All Handicapped Children Act of 1975—was remarkable in its attention to detail. Enacted at a time when executive prerogatives were viewed with suspicion and problems of implementation were thought best handled at the legislative stage, the bill prescribed with unusual exactitude the expectations for local school district officials. As a result, the program, although politically popular, has come under increasing criticism from local officials, who complain that the resources needed to implement the law far outstrip the federal dollars provided and that the administrative processes required consume inordinate amounts of time.

Policy Development

Programs for the handicapped have been proposed, and numerous pieces of legislation on their behalf have been enacted, since James Buchanan was president, some 120 years ago. But significant federal assistance for the education of the handicapped dates more recently to the Kennedy administration, which focused attention on the needs of the mentally retarded by creating a presidential panel to study the subject. Upon its recommendation, a variety of research centers, public facilities, and community mental health centers were authorized in 1963. Programs for the handicapped were also included within Title I of ESEA, vocational education programs, and an early childhood program.

During the early 1970s, there were three significant legislative developments for the handicapped. The 1973 Rehabilitation Act stated that no qualified handicapped individual could be discriminated against in the receipt of any federal assistance solely on the basis of his handicap. Then, in 1974, Congress made clear its intent to include educational programs within the provisions of the Rehabilitation Act and further included in the amendments to ESEA, passed that year, a variety of rights for handicapped children, including certain due process procedures, nondiscriminatory administration and evaluation of testing materials, and assurance of education in the least restrictive environment. But it was the 1975 legislation, the Education for All Handicapped Children Act (P.L. 94 –142), which represented the culmination of the various legislative efforts to address the needs of the handicapped, that was most significant. In addition to broadening certain educational rights for the handicapped, it authorized major federal fiscal assistance to help achieve that end.

Legislative support for P.L. 94 –142 was overwhelming in both houses of Congress, although the executive branch was critical. The Department of Health, Education, and Welfare opposed the proposal, asserting that the education of the handicapped was the responsibility of the states. President Ford warned that "its good intentions could be thwarted by the many unwise provisions it contains."[10] The president contended that authorization levels were excessive and unrealistic and that a potpourri of attached requirements would prove burdensome to effective service delivery and assert unnecessary federal control. Nonetheless, he did agree to sign the bill, which committed the federal government to:

> . . . assure that all handicapped children have available to them . . . a free appropriate public education which emphasizes special education and related services designed to meet their unique needs, to assure that the rights of handicapped children and their parents or guardians are protected, to assist States and localities to provide for the education of all handicapped children, and to assess and assure the effectiveness of efforts to educate handicapped children.[11]

As might be anticipated from the detail with which implementation of these objectives was specified, the legislation was written neither by the Office of Education nor by the major educational interest groups. Special education has for decades existed somewhat apart from and as a stepchild of the mainstream of American public education. In part, this is due to the tendency for private charities to provide services for the handicapped; in part, it is due to the lack of services provided to the handicapped through the public schools; and in part, it is due to the neglect and second-class citizenship that special educators have generally experienced. As a result, the groups most influential in shaping legislation to benefit the handicapped were not members of the so-called educational establishment, but rather the Council for Exceptional Children, the National Association for Retarded Children, and other more specialized groups concerned with the needs of the handicapped. Since these groups were generally suspicious of what schools would provide for the handicapped of their own accord, those participating in the development of the legislation considered not only questions of broad purpose but what, under other circumstances, might have been regarded as administrative details.

Neither the pressures of these groups nor the warm support of Harrison Williams, chairman of the Senate Education and Labor Committee, who encouraged his staff to develop legislation for the handicapped, would have been sufficient to pass P.L. 94 –142 had not two major court decisions been made that greatly altered the states' responsibility for the education of the handicapped. In 1971, a federal court approved a consent agreement between the Commonwealth of Pennsylvania and the Pennsylvania Association for Retarded Children, which provided that the state may not deny any mentally retarded child a free public program of education and training appropriate to the child's capacity. In light of evidence presented in court proceedings, which showed that retarded children could benefit from education, the state agreed to disregard its laws excluding mentally retarded children from a public education and to provide training appropriate to each child's capacity.

The following year, a similar case was filed against the Board of Education of the District of Columbia, which also was decided in favor of the plaintiff. In this case, the school board had denied mentally retarded children admission to the public schools and, in other instances, had suspended and expelled pupils whom the school board felt it was unable to serve. The district court issued a "declaration of constitutional rights of all children, regardless of any exceptional condition or handicap, to a publicly supported education."[12] The court explicitly rejected the school board's claim that inadequate financial resources precluded the provision of services to the handicapped. According to the judge, "The District of Columbia's interest in educating the excluded children clearly must outweigh its interest in preserving its financial resources."[13] The court reasoned that, if the schools had insufficient financial resources, limitations on school programs should apply to all children and not bear particularly heavily on the handicapped.

In light of these court decisions, and numerous cases pending in many other states, local school officials became increasingly concerned that special education costs would rapidly escalate. Since there was doubt that state and local resources would be adequate to the task, many looked to Congress to provide a way to avoid a major fiscal crisis. The Education for All Handicapped Children Act, although criticized by President Ford for the detail of its provisions, was generally welcomed by all in the educational community.

The new fiscal demands created by these court decisions also account for the rapid increase in appropriations for the handicapped that occurred before the passage of P.L. 94-142. What had been a $93 million program in 1972 became an $814 million program in 1980; President Carter's proposals for 1982 exceeded $1.2 billion. The rapid expansion of public support for special education was anticipated in the 1975 legislation. Federal support for the handicapped—unlike that for the bilingual education programs, which received funding only as "demonstration" projects—was authorized on an indefinite basis, and the legislation provided for increasing levels of support with every passing year, until eventually it was assumed that Congress would pay for 40 percent of the additional expenditure required to provide special education to every child.

As the federal share of expenditures increased, so did the number of children identified as handicapped by the public schools. By 1979, almost four million handicapped children were being served by the program (see Figure 5-1), and it is expected that this figure will con-

Figure 5-1 School-Age Handicapped Receiving Special Education[a]

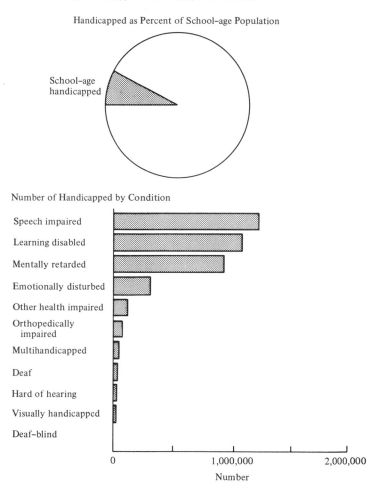

Handicapped as Percent of School-age Population

Number of Handicapped by Condition

Source: Department of Education, National Center for Education Statistics, *The Condition of Education*
         (Washington, D.C.: Government Printing Office, 1980).
         a. The handicapped who receive special education through P.L. 94-142 and P.L. 89-313 represent
         almost four million persons, or 8 percent of the total school-age population.

tinue to grow, since estimates of the number of handicapped children range anywhere from 4.9 to 10.2 million.[14] In fact, one of the difficulties in implementing the program is identifying children in need of special education services.

Because the number of handicapped children in the program has grown, the range of services provided has widened, and the cost of these services has increased. Even the large increase in federal support falls short of what Congress originally authorized and of what groups representing the handicapped continue to demand. Instead of paying 40 percent of the additional costs of special education, the federal contribution was only about 14 percent in 1976–77.[15] Many local schools complain that Congress mandated special education for all handicapped children, promised to help support such education, instituted procedures to ensure that all handicapped children are being served, but left to state and local governments much of the burden of financing the additional services required. As a result, fiscal concerns have dominated the politics of implementing P.L. 94–142.

Policy Implementation

While P.L. 94–142 has increased the availability of special education services to handicapped children, it has also significantly increased state and local costs. First, the law requires that for every child in the program, an "individualized educational program" (IEP) must be prepared at a meeting that includes representatives of the district, professionals with knowledge of the child's needs, a parent or guardian, and, when appropriate, the child himself. At these conferences, the group assesses the child's present level of educational performance and agrees upon the goals to be achieved during the coming year, the specific educational services to be provided for the child, the duration of time over which services are to be provided, and evaluative criteria and procedures to be used.

While this kind of individual attention to the needs of every child is laudable, the costs of compliance are not small. Hours of staff time are consumed when several educational professionals attend even a single meeting for each of the nearly four million pupils in special education. Numerous detailed forms must be prepared at these meetings, and as an added safety measure against legal claims that might be brought later, many of these meetings are being tape-recorded by school officials. What once might have been handled informally by telephone now requires complex, formal, time-consuming bureaucratic procedures. As one special education teacher stated, "The time factor is our biggest concern and it's getting worse. I'm out of class a lot of the time writing IEPs and I'm spending more time with parents."[16]

Whether the quality of services has improved as a result of such processes is unknown. One study noted that, in the initial years of the program, the services recommended were more a function of resources available than of the special disabilities suffered by the child. But this same study team later reported that, as special education resources expanded, schools were better able to fit educational programs to the needs of the child.[17] On the other hand, the study also found that even in 1979–80, "little change was evident in the involvement of parents. Their participation remained mostly superficial and pro forma rather than substantive."[18]

While there may not be much parent participation, P.L. 94–142 gives parents the right to examine all relevant records and the right to written notice whenever the school district intends to initiate or change services for their children. Parents also have, by law, a right to an impartial hearing in the presence of someone other than an employee of the state whenever they file a formal complaint. These procedural safeguards not only protect parents against arbitrary decisions by faceless bureaucrats, but they also have been a means by which some parents have been able to win substantially increased services for their children. In California, for example, the state cannot explicitly refuse to provide services on the basis of excessive costs (such grounds were ruled unconstitutional by federal courts), and many hearings examiners have ruled favorably on parents' complaints, requiring the provision of costly services in addition to those that were agreed upon in the individualized educational plan.[19]

School districts are also required to place children in the least restrictive environment consistent with the special needs of the child. Supporters of this provision have hoped that this requirement would move many handicapped pupils out of separate educational programs into the educational "mainstream," where they would come into regular contact with nonhandicapped children. But many teachers have expressed concern that handicapped children in regular classrooms consume disproportionate amounts of the teachers' time, and the American Federation of Teachers has stated a large number of conditions (including reductions in class size) that must be met before they can fully endorse the practice of mainstreaming.[20] Since the costs of these proposed changes are prohibitive, this federal requirement has been less effectively implemented than others. As a major study of program implementation observed, "Consideration of LRE [least restrictive environment] in the placement of special education students does not match the intent of the law as yet."[21]

Summary

Programs for the handicapped have expanded more rapidly in the past decade than any other educational program. This is due not only to vigorous lobbying efforts by special groups, but also to recent court decisions and widespread public support. Nonetheless, the legislation passed by Congress prescribed in such detail the procedures to be followed in developing special education programs that state and local officials, concerned about the 14.3 percent annual increase in the cost of these programs between 1975 and 1979,[22] have tried to determine whether further program expansion can be limited. Resource problems are likely to get worse in the 1980s. If federal funding is cut as program costs mount, as the number of children identified as handicapped grows, and as the range of required services expands, state and local governments will suffer significant financial pressures. Court decisions preclude a return to depending on private charities or other state agencies to meet the educational needs of handicapped children, as was the case prior to 1970. If a fiscal crisis develops in education in the 1980s, it will be most noticeable, it seems, in the area of special education.

Emergency School Aid Act

The concept of equal educational opportunity not only legitimated new programs for the handicapped, it also provided an umbrella under which the federal government, for the first time, assisted school districts undergoing school desegregation. Once again, judicial decisions provided the context for policy innovation. But in contrast to bilingual and special education programs, legislative initiatives that led to the Emergency School Aid Act (ESAA) did not result from interest group pressures and congressional subcommittees. The problem involved in school desegregation, and in the busing of pupils to achieve that end, had become so central to American political debate that innovations in this area were the result of broad political strategies on the part of the nation's leading politicians.

Although the program won the backing of leaders from both political parties, this by no means assured the stable constituency necessary for easy identification of objectives and smooth implementation of goals. Instead, the program was subject to shifting coalitions of support and heavy criticism from both left and right; it also became the vehicle for many a pet political project. There have been attempts to use the program to achieve higher levels of desegregation than intended, on the one side; on the other, implementation of the policy has been disrupted by various provisions and amendments that limit the program's effectiveness simply as a means to desegregate local school districts.

Policy Development

When the Nixon administration assumed office in 1969, it recognized a number of difficulties in pursuing what had become known as its "southern strategy." It was committed to minimizing civil-rights enforcement practices that treated the South differently from other parts of the United States, but realized that its efforts to achieve this goal through judicial appointments would be slow and, for a period of time, not readily apparent. Even after the appointment of Warren Burger as chief justice of the Supreme Court, the Court reaffirmed its strong commitment to school desegregation in *Alexander v. Holmes* (1969); meanwhile, numerous lower court decisions were continuing to hasten school desegregation in the South. In fact, it was precisely during the first years of the Nixon administration that the greatest racial changes in school attendance patterns were occurring.

Unable to halt court-ordered desegregation, the Nixon administration, in a well-conceived plan designed to maintain credibility among civil-rights leaders and to win support in the South, developed a desegregation policy along the following lines: to express regularly the administration's opposition to judicial activism; to make more conservative appointments to the courts whenever possible; to slow the executive administrative machinery responsible for desegregation enforcement; and to provide financial assistance to those districts forced to undergo school desegregation.

This last plank in the policy, which was the basis for ESAA, was inserted "at the last moment" into the president's March 1970 statement on school desegregation. Nixon observed in this presentation that "successfully desegregating the nation's schools requires more than the enforcement of laws. It also requires investment of money."[23] Nixon proposed expenditure of $500 million in fiscal year 1971 and $1 billion in fiscal year 1972 in the following areas:

> Aid to districts now eliminating de jure segregation. . . . Aid to districts that wish to undertake voluntary efforts to eliminate, reduce or prevent de facto racial isolation. . . . Aid for the purpose of helping establish special or intercultural education programs or . . . designed to overcome the educational disadvantages that stem from racial isolation.[24]

All grants to such districts were to be made for specific projects and required the approval of the secretary of Health, Education, and Welfare (HEW). Two-thirds of the funds were to be allotted among the states by a formula based on the proportion of the nation's minority students located in each state. Minority students residing in districts required by law to desegregate would be counted twice. The remaining one-third of the funds could be allocated by the HEW secretary for especially promising projects in any eligible district.

Civil-rights supporters and school officials initially supported the Nixon proposal, but their enthusiasm cooled considerably when Nixon attached a new provision that prohibited use of the money for busing; "This, in effect, dissociated the administration from busing, and it was strongly opposed by school officials and civil rights groups and provoked new battles in Congress."[25] Republican Senator Jacob Javits expressed reluctance to introduce the bill because of the antibusing language. Eventually, the White House dropped the provision but reserved the right to reintroduce it at a later date;[26] this facilitated the appropriation of $75 million on an emergency, "interim" basis, while deliberations on the full proposal continued. Democratic opposition focused on the plan to double-count children in school districts forced to desegregate by court order, since this was perceived as allocating a disproportionate amount of funds to the South. Representative Carl Perkins contended that there was no need for such a bill, as it would unnecessarily duplicate funding made available through the Elementary and Secondary Education Act of 1965.[27]

Despite Perkins's opposition, the House moved more rapidly than the Senate to endorse the proposal, and the House Education and Labor Committee reported the ESAA proposal to the floor on November 30, 1970. The committee dropped the double-counting provision and reduced the funding for special projects from 33 to 20 percent. The House required that 90 percent of ESAA funds be allocated on the basis of the formula, further limiting HEW discretion over special grants to just 10 percent of the total funds approved. The House voted 159–77 in favor of ESAA.

Interestingly, opposition came from the most conservative and the most liberal members of the House. The conservatives were guided by Ohio Republican John Ashbrook, who contended that ESAA was not an "emergency program" but a "new and permanent program of dubious value." He and his conservative colleagues argued that the legislation "would put Congress clearly on the record as favoring a massive, federally aided school busing program."[28] The liberals asserted that much of the money would be "squandered" and allocated to districts unwilling to desegregate. Their point was underscored in early 1971 when the General Accounting Office released a report demonstrating that more than 90 percent of the interim funds had been allocated to states in the South.

These concerns prevented Senate consideration of the bill before the end of the Ninety-first Congress. Undaunted, the Nixon administration reintroduced the legislation, largely unchanged, in early 1971. The legislation did not mention transportation of students in desegregation efforts; it recommended that 80 percent of the funds be allocated by formula, with the remainder earmarked for special projects. Leading Senate liberals—including Walter Mondale, Edward Kennedy, Hubert Humphrey, George McGovern, Edward Brooke, and Edmund Muskie—responded with an alternative bill that focused expenditure more specifically on desegregation-related costs. A compromise was achieved, and both Houses approved the legislation as part of the Higher Education Act of 1972.

While the ESAA that was approved and signed into law in June 1972 resembled the proposal first introduced by the Nixon administration, it was altered in some respects. The final bill divided a substantial amount of the funding into a number of quite specific areas reflecting the particular concerns of influential members of Congress. Special grants were set aside for pilot compensatory programs, metropolitan area projects such as educational parks, bilingual education programs, educational television, and special assistance to private groups and to public agencies other than school boards. The remainder of the ESAA funds were to be distributed among the states on the basis of a formula, largely determined by the number of minority group children of school age. The legislation did not specifically prohibit use of ESAA funds for busing, but the Department of Health, Education, and Welfare generally denied allocation for such purposes.

In 1974, when ESAA came up for congressional reconsideration, there was, once again, heated debate over busing. President Nixon, who initially proposed the act, requested that Congress permit it to expire. He put forward instead a smaller program for "selected school districts facing critical problems as a result of either mandatory or voluntary desegregation."[29] Congress ignored this proposal and extended ESAA for an additional two years, although it "prohibited spending the desegregation money for busing and also denied local officials discretion to use money from most other federal programs for this purpose."[30] Congress remained supportive of ESAA in face of President Ford's recommendation that funding be dramatically reduced. When Ford vetoed the appropriation for ESAA, both houses responded with an override in the summer of 1975. When ESAA was extended again in 1978, HEW was given greater discretion over the distribution of funds and magnet schools, which were expected to attract an integrated clientele voluntarily by the quality of their educational offerings, were embraced as an additional special grant category.

ESAA funding continued to increase throughout the 1970s. It climbed from $92.2 million in fiscal year 1972 to $204 million in fiscal year 1976 to $304.5 million in fiscal year 1980 (see Table 3-1). But when examined in constant dollars, ESAA funding peaked around fiscal year 1976 (see Table 3-2). From the beginning, the program was buffeted by political controversy and was the object of special claims. As is shown in Table 5-3, the rate at which amendments were offered to ESAA on the floors of the House and Senate was more than double the rate on any other piece of legislation on education. It was completely eliminated as a distinctive program in the first year of the Reagan administration.

Policy Implementation

The multiple and somewhat contradictory forces that shaped ESAA legislation affected the way in which the program was implemented. While the program assisted school districts undergoing desegregation in all parts of the United States, restrictions on the distribution of funds precluded concentration of resources where the need was greatest. As a result, the overall distribution of resources was only loosely related to program objectives.

According to a major study carried out five years after the program had been authorized, ESAA funds had been received by "less than one-half of the districts known to have had high reductions in minority isolation"; at the same time, 14 percent of all districts—and 40 percent of the districts in the North and West—that received a basic grant under the program "did not reduce the number or percent of minority

Table 5-3 Amendments to Education Bills Offered on Floors of House and Senate, 1960-79

Legislative Subject	Average Number of Amendments Offered per Year Since Program First Was Introduced
Emergency school aid	10.2
ESEA Title I	4.9
Bilingual	.6
Handicapped	2.0
Impact aid	4.0
Vocational education	.8
NDEA III and subsequent legislation	.4

Source: *Congressional Quarterly Almanac* (1960-79).

pupils in minority isolation to any degree."[31] In other words, funds were being given to many districts that were not integrating, while many districts carrying out a desegregation plan were not receiving funds.

There are several reasons for this disjunction in resource allocation. In the first place, "a large number of . . . potentially eligible districts have not applied for ESAA grants . . . [because of a] dislike for OCR [Office of Civil Rights] compliance reviews."[32] In addition, many local officials have discovered that the uses to which the monies can be applied are restricted in critical ways. Not only does the law prohibit use of the monies for purposes of transporting pupils, one of the most expensive costs to a school district that adopts a plan for integration, but it further provides that funds may not be used for purposes that are part of the integration plan itself. Instead, funds are to be used only to deal with problems that arise as a result of desegregation. Thus, for example, if a federal judge orders a district to provide compensatory education as part of its desegregation plan, ESAA funds cannot be used for this purpose. If, on the other hand, no such provision is included in the desegregation plan, ESAA funds can be used for compensatory education. Over the years, local school officials, working in cooperation with federal judges, have become quite successful in working out agreements that allow maximum use of federal funds, but these and other peculiarities of federal guidelines have discouraged many districts from participating in the program.

Another reason why funds do not always go to districts undergoing desegregation is that the allocation of funds among the states is determined by a formula based on the number of minority pupils within states. When funding requests are received, the impact of the proposed services on reducing minority isolation and on improving learning environments is evaluated, but the major determinant of fund distribution is the number of minority students living within the district. By itself, this is not a measure of school desegregation.

Once districts receive ESAA funds, they do seem able to turn these monies into additional school resources. Schools in ESAA basic programs had significantly greater per pupil supplemental allocations for reading and mathematics instruction and were more likely to use remedial specialists and instructional aides. Also, one study found that, in the third year of the program, pupils in schools participating in ESAA showed greater achievement gains than those in a sample of schools not included in the program. The findings from this study are unusually impressive,[33] since schools were assigned to treatment and control groups on a random basis.

Summary

These difficulties with ESAA are a function of the context in which the legislation was conceived. ESAA was at once a civil-rights initiative and a policy designed to slow desegregation. A compromise between left and right, it was hardly likely to allocate funds efficiently. The major surprise, in fact, was ESAA's political resilience over the short term. Despite initial congressional reluctance to pass the proposal, and later executive branch efforts to gut it, ESAA provided support for school desegregation until 1981. And during Republican administrations, "the desegregation requirements [in ESAA] were so unambiguous that HEW continued enforcing them long after it stopped enforcing the Civil Rights Act."[34] But ESAA was terminated in 1981, when the Reagan administration succeeded in blending the program into its block-grant proposals. While compensatory education, bilingual education, and special education all escaped this fate, support for ESAA was too diffuse, too politically based, and insufficiently rooted in a specific, well-organized interest group to spare it from the block-grant drive.

Conclusions

Ever since the passage of the Elementary and Secondary Education Act in 1965, equal educational opportunity has been a powerful motivating force for federal policy. Apart from Title I of ESEA itself, the concept has legitimated demands for bilingual education, special education for the handicapped, and special assistance to schools undergoing school desegregation. Moreover, it has been the basis for significant legislative changes in vocational education programs and has even affected impact aid policies. Demands for a reduction in sex bias and sex stereotyping in education have also been advanced under this umbrella, and as a result, the Office of Civil Rights within the Department of Education has required significant changes in vocational and extracurricular programming. Finally, equal opportunity has been the ground on which many have attempted to bring about financial reforms in the educational systems in many states.

Apart from this last movement, most of the efforts to improve equal opportunity have been addressed to the federal government. That has not been an accident. Both state governments and local school districts operate under economic and political constraints that make it much more difficult for them to respond favorably to demands for equal opportunity. Local governments cannot spend more than their relatively inelastic tax revenues provide. The more they concentrate services on low-income groups, the more they discourage capital investments that are essential to preserving their tax bases.

These inadequacies at the local level have brought to the federal government numerous demands for equalizing educational opportunities. As a result, federal education policy, although formulated haphazardly and in response to ad hoc group and partisan pressures, has had a particular emphasis that distinguishes it both from pre–1965 federal programs that had little focus and few regulations and from state and local programs less attentive to equal access questions.

But while the focus on equal opportunity has given overall direction to federal education policy, Congress and the Department of Education have been less clear about ways in which they can achieve that objective without interfering in educational practices best left to local determination. As each categorical program has defined equal opportunity in its own way, the Department of Education has developed another set of regulations designed to implement that vision. This chapter has shown how a number of these regulations have needlessly involved national administrators in local decisions, placed substantial administrative burdens on local officials, and escalated fiscal pressures on local governments. Chapter 6 will explore the ways in which categorical educational programs have begun to duplicate, overlap, and contradict one another, thereby even more directly raising the question, how can the federal government better achieve its distinctive interest in equal educational opportunity while at the same time encouraging states and localities to provide the highest possible quality educational programs?

SEEKING A BALANCED FEDERAL ROLE

The establishment of a Department of Education in 1980 made inescapable the presence of a federal education policy. While no single coherent statement of that policy exists, the federal government, since the passage of the Elementary and Secondary Education Act (ESEA) in 1965, has developed a set of purposes under the broad theme of equal opportunity. In contrast to earlier federal involvement in education, which asked localities to do little except what was already integral to their operations, this set of purposes was distinct from those that state and local governments typically had pursued. At the same time, new rules and regulations emerged that, while part and parcel of the new objectives, encumbered local school districts in a variety of ways.

There is growing concern about this new federal role, just as there is growing discontent about the way in which the nation's public schools educate. As shown earlier, current federal policies promote supplemental programs, providing resources to meet the needs of special groups within the population instead of supplying funds for general use by the school districts. Further, federal policies do not establish educational standards and objectives. Some observers blame these policies for many of the perceived problems in the education system; they believe that federal policy, far from improving educational quality, has had a negative impact.

Debate over the future direction of federal policy has centered on two distinct but not unrelated questions. The first is how to raise educational standards. Some argue that the federal government, by enunciating basic standards and distributing funds on the condition that these standards be met, could clarify local educational objectives. Others claim that school performances can be raised—and brought closer to parental expectations—by increasing the competition among local schools. This chapter will examine whether either of these approaches provides an appropriate focus for federal policy. The second question over which policymakers are divided is whether or not it is desirable to substitute a block grant for the potpourri of categorical programs currently in existence. Those advocating block grants insist that only categorical grants will maintain equal educational opportunity. This chapter will investigate the merits of the arguments offered by both sides and search for a middle position that recognizes the most valid claims of each.

Maintaining Educational Standards

Two fundamentally different strategies for improving educational standards have surfaced in recent years. The first—competency-based education (CBE)—maintains that standards can be raised only through more central direction and control. The second—maximizing parental choice—claims that standards can be raised only if schools must compete with one another for consumer loyalty in a competitive marketplace. Neither of these strategies is entirely satisfactory. There is considerable merit, however, in a tuition voucher or tax credit plan that would allow students greater choice among high schools. Current programs are least effective at this level of education, and the institutional arrangements in higher education may provide a model for the future direction of the American high school.

Competency-Based Education

For some, the case against current federal policy is not that there is too much regulation but the wrong kind; they perceive the sins of federal policy not as ones of commission but of omission. According to some indicators, student performances at the secondary-school level fell steadily in the 1970s. While this trend may be attributable to the growing number of single-parent families, the weakening of parental influence over adolescent behavior, teenagers' substitution of television-watching for reading, declining college admission standards, and simplified high-school texts,[1] it may also be the result of a failure on the part of federal policy to address the question of educational standards. Has the federal government's focus on equality of education prevented it from attending to the equally critical matter of educational excellence?

While improving the quality of American education has become a national concern, this is one of many questions not readily resolved by a single, federally imposed set of regulations. Corrective actions may be more effective if taken by individual school districts, schools of education, colleges and universities, and state legislatures. And evidence is accumulating that state and local authorities are attempting to address the problem of falling standards. For example, without the guidance of any well-organized group or any educational leader of stature, and in the face of opposition from organized teacher groups, the CBE movement has swept across the United States like a prairie fire; CBE programs have been inaugurated in thirty-six states.[2]

As is often the case in a highly decentralized system of education, these programs vary in conception and implementation in different parts of the country. In some places, the emphasis is on student performance, with standards specified for graduation from high school. In other places, the emphasis is on curricular guidelines and accompanying tests. Programs also vary in the extent to which curricula and tests are centrally or locally prepared. The subject matters in which competency is required also differ from one state to the next, including such diverse topics as consumer economics, citizenship, survival skills, spelling, social studies, government and economics, everyday living skills, health and drugs, communications, social responsibility, career development, problem solving, reasoning, listening, history, free enterprise, and cultures of the United States.[3]

In general, however, "what has come to be called CBE is [typically] a testing and remediation program focused on basic literacy and mathematical skills."[4] One example of such a program is that administered by the state of Florida, which holds a statewide test in which students must demonstrate minimum competencies prior to receipt of a high-school diploma. In all, seventeen states now require that high-school students pass some kind of a test before they are granted a diploma. In some places, a single test is given upon completion of high school; in other places, tests are administered at the end of each academic year to make sure that students are steadily building competencies as they move from one grade to the next.

Although CBE undertakings vary greatly in focus and quality, there is some evidence that they have had positive effects on student performances, as pupils have shown the greatest improvement in subjects either directly or very closely related to those in which competency tests are given. There is even some evidence that overall levels of verbal and numerical ability are slightly improved whenever both the passing of tests is required for graduation and remedial programs are in place to help students achieve basic competencies. A recent nationwide survey of high-school sophomores and seniors found modestly higher levels of proficiency in basic skills—especially in mathematics—in schools with CBE and remedial programs: "While the evidence remains weak, it does suggest that deliberate efforts by schools to ensure minimum levels of performance in basic skills by all students might in fact be productive (if only marginally so)."[5]

Those leaning toward active federal efforts to upgrade educational quality may find CBE programs of particular interest because, established by state legislatures and administered by state departments of education, they contain all of the detailed regulations, evaluation procedures, and local school compliance requirements likely to be concomitant to federal initiatives in this area. But while CBE has been popular and marginally successful in improving student performances, it has been roundly criticized by teacher organizations and local school officials for imposing narrow educational goals, administrative details, and burdensome testing procedures. Arthur Wise has voiced these complaints vigorously:

> In the drive to make educational institutions accountable, goals have become narrow, selective, and minimal. That which is measurable is preferred to that which is unmeasurable. . . . The technology of criterion-referenced testing [a constituent component of CBE] when combined with the ideology of basic skills, permits linking tests to the needs of adult life. The ideology of basic skills and the technology of criterion-referenced testing combine to allow the policy process to control the educational process. . . . Through this process, the goal of schooling is reduced to the instrumental value of providing just enough reading and arithmetic skill to get by as an adult.[6]

Were the federal government to attempt to upgrade American education, it could either provide funds for broad educational purposes with few accompanying regulations (the NDEA approach), or specify objectives that local authorities must achieve in order to become eligible for funding (something like CBE). If the federal government pursues the first approach, which is little more than a general block grant to states and localities, it incurs much less risk than if it tries the second approach, which leaves it open to all of the charges and complaints raised with respect to categoricals. Given the fact that many states and localities have already instituted CBE programs, the federal government might well wait and see how successful these efforts are before saddling itself with still another categorical program.

These considerations might explain the paucity of political support for a federal CBE program. Neither the Department of Education nor any senator or congressman with a strong interest in education has promoted a national CBE policy. Were they to do so, such a program would run contrary to the Republican party's emphasis on state and local control and to the Democratic party's concern with focusing federal programs on low-income and disadvantaged groups. While American educational standards may need upgrading, it may be politically unfeasible and extremely unwise for this effort to be undertaken by the federal government.

Increasing Parental Choice

Some observers believe that, rather than attempting to upgrade educational institutions by proclaiming nationwide standards and promulgating elaborate testing mechanisms, it may be possible to improve schools by increasing the level of competition among them. If parents and pupils can choose among a variety of schools, those schools that are successful will prosper and expand; those that are not will go bankrupt and disappear.

This idea has become increasingly popular. For example, many who operate nonpublic schools (including the Catholic church, which provides approximately 75 percent of all non-public-school education in the United States) no longer seek increased direct government assistance; instead, they favor the concept of consumer choice, aided by indirect government support through tuition-assistance schemes. A few years ago, several experiments with tuition-voucher plans were tried (with mixed success). In 1978, the House of Representatives approved a tax credit that would have allowed parents to deduct a limited amount of non-public-school tuition from their income tax. At that time, the Senate refused to go along with the House proposal, but tax credit supporters gained votes in the 1980 elections, and the Reagan administration has proposed a modest tax credit plan.

The tax credit proposal has been given a boost by a major study conducted by the well-known educational sociologist James Coleman and two associates.[7] Based on a national sample of public and nonpublic schools, the study identified differences in the performances of students in nonpublic as compared with public schools. Even after differences in the family background characteristics of students were taken into account, Coleman et al. discovered that non-public-school students performed better in verbal and numerical ability tests. The authors cited lower absenteeism, better discipline, and more demanding homework assignments in the nonpublic schools as the likely reasons for the difference in performance. Other researchers have attacked Coleman's methodology and conclusions.[8] They point out that the tests of verbal and numerical abilities were very crude, that unmeasured differences in motivation may account for the differences in performances, and that the conclusions go far beyond what can be derived from the information gathered.

But even if the core findings in the Coleman study withstand these and other criticisms, the implications for policy are more complex than they first appear. The very success of non-public-school education may depend upon the existence of a public-school system that absorbs students with emotional, disciplinary, and other problems (students who would be suspended or expelled from private schools). As the Coleman study itself observed, "The effectiveness of discipline is dependent [in part on the fact that] private schools have more control over the entrance and exit of their students than do public schools."[9] Were the government to subsidize private schools in a major way, they might well become more like public schools.

This elitist focus of many nonpublic schools is emphasized by critics of tax credit and tuition-voucher plans. According to the Coleman study, the percentage of students attending nonpublic schools increases decidedly as family income increases, and the percentage of blacks in nonpublic schools is lower at all income levels.[10] Moreover, only about 2.7 percent of nonpublic schools provide programs for the handicapped, only 3 percent provide vocational education, and only about 4.4 percent offer compensatory education.[11] On the basis of these findings, it has been said that the expansion of nonpublic education will inevitably increase class and racial segregation in education. In contrast, according to a recent Congressional Budget Office study, "Public schools must serve all comers, many of whom are difficult to control or have special educational problems that require considerable resources to overcome."[12]

Much depends on the particular characteristics of any plan for increasing parental choice. The opportunity for those less financially well-off to attend nonpublic schools could be increased if the size of tuition vouchers were in inverse proportion to family income, and if schools receiving vouchers were required to include pupils from diverse racial and social backgrounds. But enforcement of these requirements might introduce a new series of state controls over education that would destroy the autonomy and independence that seem to make many nonpublic schools so successful. Tax credits or tax deductions that provide fiscal relief for families sending their children to nonpublic schools are more likely to win congressional approval than are tuition vouchers. While these proposals have the virtue of being easily administered, they are likely to provide the greatest benefits to higher-income families. The federal government, which has for two decades attempted to equalize access to education, would now be sponsoring programs that have quite the opposite effect.

Little appreciated by either side in debates over tax credits and tuition vouchers is the extent to which parents already have a choice in the education of their children. Public schools in the United States are operated by thousands of different local school boards, which provide programs differing in curricular emphasis and organization, racial composition, and level of fiscal support. Hundreds of separate school districts may be found within a single metropolitan area; these districts compete for teachers, administrators, and "quality" students.

A growing body of research indicates that families are sensitive to differences in school quality as indicated by the so-called white flight from central-city school systems.[13] While early studies reached varying conclusions on this, it is now agreed that when central-city schools become minority-dominated and predominantly white schools exist in surrounding suburbs, white middle-class families will leave the central city in significant numbers.[14] Less well-known is the relationship between better educational services (measured either by the level of school expenditures or student test scores) and the value of a community's property. Studies show that families are willing to pay more to live in neighborhoods where there are good schools.[15]

These findings cut two ways. On the one hand, they dispel the claim of public-school supporters that tuition vouchers will undercut equal educational opportunity provided by the present system. In large metropolitan areas, the difference between central-city schools attended largely by minorities and suburban schools serving a white middle class continues to grow. Within the public-school system as it exists today, equality seems more a goal to pursue than a reality that needs to be protected. On the other hand, the findings undermine the argument of voucher supporters that choice, by itself, guarantees quality education. If choice were the key determinant of quality, there would be little complaint about public schools today. It is doubtful that tax credits or tax deductions would produce significantly greater choice than is currently provided by competing suburban school districts.

Whatever the merits of tax credits or tuition vouchers, the chances that they will be adopted on a nationwide scale remain slim. Despite the commitments of the Reagan administration, supporters of tax credits are likely to encounter many difficulties. The National Coalition for Public Education, an umbrella group for forty public-school and civil-rights organizations, has already launched a vigorous campaign against the idea. Just as similar groups were able to prevent aid to parochial schools in the 1950s, this new coalition is likely to find a way to entangle tax credit proposals in some congressional thicket. Moreover, the Reagan administration—whose top priorities have remained general tax relief, increased defense undertakings, and reduced domestic expenditures—may be less than enthusiastic about a "tax expenditure" that could cost the federal government as much as $7 billion a year. As Daniel Moynihan, a key supporter of non-public-school aid, observed in May 1981, "I looked to the 97th Congress as the one that would finally come to grips with this issue of justice. Candidly, I must report that our prospects are dimmer now."[16]

But even though tax credits cannot be offered as a panacea, they deserve consideration as a means for restructuring the American high school. By all accounts, the last three years of public school are the least successful: in these years, student performances fall most dramatically, adolescent disgust and resentment are most evident, and the purpose of schooling is most difficult to discern. Further, the value of the high-school diploma in the marketplace is decreasing; high-school grades and teachers' recommendations carry less weight with college admissions officers than do SAT scores; and the comprehensive high school, by attempting to cater to the interests of all, satisfies no one. Significantly, many of the most successful high schools in large central cities are those that have narrowed their scope and purpose—the vocational schools, performing arts schools, and magnet schools, which are increasingly preferred over the once popular neighborhood schools that in many cases are more dominated by peer group culture than by any well-defined adult purpose.

Choice is already the hallmark of postsecondary institutions. At the age of seventeen or eighteen, young people are given a plethora of options that range from private college to state university, from junior college to vocational training center. Escape from secondary schools to these more purposeful institutions is so attractive that many students complete their high-school degree program outside the secondary school. At a time when teenagers are becoming more mobile and independent, they need to be given a greater sense of autonomy in their schooling. A growing number of students now attend schools without walls (high-school programs that draw on resources throughout the city instead of limiting themselves to what is available in any one school building), participate in career training programs, and travel long distances from home to attend a school of their choice. If a tuition voucher or tax credit arrangement facilitated still more choice and differentiation in secondary education, schools might become more responsive to the social, educational, and vocational needs of young adults.

Categorical versus Block Grant Programming

The Case for Block Grants

Many critics of the current federal role argue that educational policy is best left to state and local officials. According to a recent report of the conservative Heritage Foundation: "Local authority has always been one of the greatest strengths of our educational system. . . . Local school officials must certainly know the needs of their students better than the federal government."[17] It follows, then, that any federal assistance to localities should be distributed with a minimum of regulations and administrative controls. The Reagan administration initially proposed, before some congressional modification, two block grants in education—one to the states and one directly to local school districts—to be distributed with minimal accompanying regulations. An administration spokesman explained, "The federal role is to supply necessary resources, not to specify in excruciating detail what must be done with these resources."[18]

While a general commitment to local control over education undergirds the thinking of those in favor of block grants, the following specific criticisms of existing categorical grants deserve careful attention: (1) categoricals have encouraged local administrators to become increasingly concerned about procedural questions, even at the expense of substantive educational needs; (2) categoricals mandate overlapping programs administered according to contradictory criteria; (3) categoricals fragment the delivery of educational services; and (4) categoricals have so magnified the schools' concern for the disadvantaged that mainline programs serving middle-class pupils have deteriorated.

Categoricals have encouraged local administrators to become increasingly concerned about procedural questions, even at the expense of substantive educational needs. By law, the federal government is forbidden from directly ordering any particular educational curriculum or teaching practice. As a result, federal regulations have focused on such procedural questions as parent and student rights, equal access, and the due process administration of individual cases.

Title I requirements, for example, instruct local administrators to concentrate resources on disadvantaged children in schools serving low-income areas. Compliance requires that local administrators keep detailed records on the way in which Title I schools are selected, the way in which state and local funds are allocated among schools throughout the district, and the social and educational backgrounds of participants in the program. To comply with Title VII, administrators must ascertain the native tongue of every child in the school system, must establish formal criteria for admission to bilingual education programs, and must see to it that a sufficient number of English-speaking students are participating in bilingual classes. P.L. 94–142, which finances programs for the handicapped, requires local preparation of an individualized educational plan for every pupil, parental involvement in the preparation of that plan, and notification to parents of their right to challenge any feature of that plan in due process hearings. These examples illustrate, but by no means exhaust, the array of federal procedural requirements under which local authorities labor.

Apart from demonstrating compliance with federal guidelines, local officials must also participate regularly in a host of evaluation activities. As already discussed, the federal government requires that, when funds are provided for Title I, bilingual education, programs for the handicapped, and vocational training, tests must be administered—in most cases both at the beginning and at the end of the school year—for purposes of program evaluation. Sometimes tests are also administered to "control groups" not directly involved in federal programming. Local educational authorities must allocate considerable resources to prepare the exams, administer them, compile the results, and interpret the findings, even though most local officials see little of value in the effort. These federal requirements have led to what Arthur Wise has called "hyperrationalization" in American education:

> When the policy objective is to promote fair treatment, new procedures such as adversarial due process hearings are introduced. When the policy objective is to promote equal treatment, new rules governing, for example, resource allocation are introduced. When the policy objective is to promote effectiveness, goals are prescribed by such techniques as competency-based education. When the policy objective is to promote efficiency, scientific management procedures such as PPBS [Policy, Planning, and Budgeting Systems] are prescribed. Although the objectives are usually salutary, the policies frequently do not have their intended effects and sometimes have unintended effects. They often represent the misapplication of legal, scientific, and management rationality to education. And they often introduce a pernicious concern for quasi-legal procedures, arbitrary rules, measurable outcomes, and pseudoscientific process.[19]

This focus on procedure in American education is hardly new. In the nineteenth century, when state aid was first distributed on the basis of the number of children in average daily attendance, school districts made up elaborate procedures for ascertaining which children were in school. Attendance-taking still consumes a significant portion of the school day. For decades, schools have also complied with complex pro-

cedural requirements that affect the ways in which textbooks are selected, materials ordered, and teachers recruited. Any enterprise that must
demonstrate to the public that it is operating honestly, efficiently, and
fairly must follow procedures that can seem annoyingly complicated to
those directly involved.[20]

Increases in procedural requirements during the past decade are at
least as much due to changing judicial policies as to new congressional
legislation. Quite apart from the school desegregation cases, which
have focused attention on the racial composition of schools, numerous
questions of individual rights, equal access, and due process in education have received the attention of the courts. Due process considerations increasingly govern the school dress code and the manner in
which disciplinary action is taken. Parental consent is needed before a
child can participate in class trips, attend special school functions, or
participate in remedial instruction. Equal access must be given to girls
interested in sports, to minorities seeking instruction in their own language, and to the handicapped asking for instruction appropriate to
their needs. Much of the increase in federal involvement in education
in the past decade is attributable to changed expectations created by
court decisions.[21]

Procedural requirements also have been the by-product of changes
in states' laws. Some of the new state-mandated requirements parallel
those of the federal government. For example, twenty-three states
administer some kind of compensatory education program, twenty
states have their own bilingual education programs, and numerous
states have liberalized their special education programs in the past ten
years.[22] In addition, the states have moved forward in one area that
federal policymakers have largely ignored: competency-based education. Proceduralism in American education is thus long-standing and
pervasive. A public institution cannot be held accountable either to its
constituents or to its administrative and political leaders without using
bureaucratic forms and practices.

As society becomes more complex and increasingly sensitive to
questions of individual rights, due process, and equal access, procedural requirements are certain to expand. While Congress has contributed to this trend in American education, it is doubtful that block
grants will restore the simplicities and informalities associated with the
romantic conception of teaching and learning in the little red schoolhouse.

*Categoricals mandate overlapping programs administered according
to contradictory criteria.* While this complaint was particularly valid in
the early years of categorical programs, more recently, many instances
of overlap and contradiction have been worked out through incremen-

tal modification of federal law and regulations. For example, at one time, state compensatory education programs were regarded by Title I administrators as part of the basic state and local allocation among schools. As a result, school districts were not permitted to use state compensatory funds for programs in schools located in fairly low-income, low-achieving areas that nonetheless failed to qualify for Title I funds. They were required instead to spend state funds on the same schools that received Title I funding. Many local officials felt this extraordinarily generous treatment of a few schools, which benefited from both state and federal programs, created problems of equality. Fortunately, statutory changes passed in 1978 greatly mitigated this difficulty and have permitted much closer coordination between state and federal compensatory programs; in California, for example, one application can be made by local school districts for both programs.

In some areas, however, contradictions persist. One especially difficult problem stems from the various meanings given to the phrase "equal educational opportunity." In some contexts, it is thought to mean both the identical treatment of all pupils and the intermingling of children from diverse backgrounds. Based on this definition, efforts have been made by both Justice and Education Department officials to desegregate local schools, and requirements have been passed to ensure that bilingual education programs include pupils whose native tongue is English and that handicapped children are educated in the least restrictive environment feasible. But other federal programs imply that equal educational opportunity requires special treatment of minorities: Title I procedures encourage local school districts to select economically and educationally disadvantaged children for special treatment, bilingual education programs encourage the isolation of non-English-speaking children from other ethnic groups, and schools have found it difficult to desegregate while retaining their Title I status. As the authors of one analysis have written:

> A number of federal programs generate *conflicting signals* for local and state program administrators. For example, the combined force of the fiscal controls in the Title I regulations and legislation strongly encourages schools to pull students out of their regular classrooms for Title I instruction. Bilingual classes are also separate from monolingual classes. Not only do these practices raise serious worries about the ill effects of tracking, segregation, and limited communication between special and regular teachers, they are also the opposite of the strategy mandated for handicapped children.[23]

These competing strategies reflect the larger dilemma of how to resolve group differences in a pluralistic society. Each course has its strengths and limitations. The first strategy—integrating individuals across group lines—increases social cohesion and maximizes individual opportunity. But integration progresses slowly and often at the expense of the minority group culture. In addition, the needs of many individual members of the minority may not be addressed during the long process of "mainstreaming." The second strategy—treating each group separately but equally—affirms the legitimacy and dignity of all groups in a pluralistic society, allowing each group to maintain its own traditions. Many multinational societies—Belgium, India, and Canada are well-known examples—seek with varying degrees of success to equalize opportunities through explicit recognition of group differences. But, as the history of school segregation since *Plessy v. Ferguson* reveals, it is difficult to sustain policies of "separate but equal." Institutions serving minorities are likely to have less esteem, fewer resources, and to use their resources less effectively. In the end, separate but equal policies may only legitimate and reinforce existing inequalities.

In the United States, the choice between these two paths to equality of opportunity has not yet been made. While the Supreme Court's *Brown v. Board of Education* decision pushed the nation toward the first strategy, the second approach is implied by the Court's *Lau v. Nichols* decision. Moreover, the growing political participation of a Spanish-speaking minority more interested in cultural parity than social integration has further encouraged the country to explore the possibilities of this second course.

Until the fundamental political choice is made between these two paths toward equality of opportunity, it is unlikely that contradictions in educational programs will be resolved. Some programs, supported by one faction, will continue to push toward integration; other programs, backed by cultural pluralists, will head off in quite another direction. Furthermore, calls for consistency may be misplaced. In the end, there may not be one best way to bring about social integration and cohesion; a certain amount of ambiguity in educational policy may be appropriate, given society's ambivalence with respect to these complex issues.

Categorical programs fragment the delivery of educational services. Traditionally, the assignment of responsibility within the education system—especially at the elementary-school level—has been "territorial." That is, teachers were responsible for the overall development of a class of children; principals were expected to care for all aspects of their neighborhood school; and deputy superintendents, to whom the principals reported, were responsible for the school district. (In large cities, the principal would report to a subdistrict or area superintendent, who also had a clear territorial jurisdiction.)

This division of responsibility was based on the assumption that the processes of learning were so complex and interconnected that they could not be divided into their component parts for specialized attention. For example, young children were thought to need attention by teachers who understood the interrelationships among their physical, emotional, and intellectual well-being. It was also assumed that general teaching skills, not specialized knowledge, were most relevant for learning.

As educational systems have become more complex, this territorial division of responsibilities has been modified by an alternative functional principle of organization. As early as the nineteenth century, secondary schools called for departmentalization as special expertise was thought relevant to successful teaching. Over the years, schools have acquired vocational teachers, music and art teachers, librarians, guidance counselors, curriculum experts, reading specialists, resource teachers (who advise classroom teachers on instructional techniques), and special educators for the handicapped. At both secondary- and elementary-school levels, the duties of "regular" classroom teachers have been defined more narrowly, while additional specialists assumed increasing numbers of tasks. The principal's coordinating function has greatly expanded, perhaps at the expense of the more traditional responsibility for setting the educational tone and providing leadership to the local school.

Specialization proliferated, especially at the high-school level. Central office curriculum experts assumed responsibility for program innovations in areas of their particular expertise. Directors of vocational training identified the equipment and materials needed for vocational programs and assumed responsibility for evaluating teachers for various vocational subspecialties. Districtwide administrative officers assumed authority over such areas as guidance counseling, testing and evaluation, medical services, and special education for the handicapped. While in most school districts these specialists are considered staff, thereby leaving authority in the hands of deputy or area superintendents and school principals, in practice, the relationships among functional specialists, who have similar training, licensing, and career expectations, often become more closely knit than relationships that had developed out of territorial propinquity.

Federal policy undoubtedly accentuated the transformation of education from a network of little red schoolhouses to a complex system of functionally differentiated activities. Federal and state vocational programs, with their accompanying regulations, helped create the relatively autonomous world of vocational education, which has its own licensing practices, journals, research centers, and administrative hierarchy. In the early years of the National Defense and Education Act (NDEA) program, a similar pattern began to emerge in the teaching of science and mathematics.

With the advent of Title I, the trend toward increasing specialization was encouraged in three ways. First, the program called for the recruitment of new, specialized personnel—including evaluators, reading specialists, and teacher aides—considered desirable not only because they could concentrate on Title I objectives but also because their presence established the fact that Title I programs were supplemental to regular classroom programming. Second, because Title I programs had to be administered according to federal and state guidelines, a separate administrative staff was needed at school site, district office, and state levels. In many districts, this administrative staff, supported by special federal funding, became a quasi-autonomous group, separate from the rest of the administrative system. Third, Title I required parental involvement in program development, and in many communities these parent groups—which proved to be quite influential—helped to sustain the separate identity of programs for the disadvantaged.

What has been characteristic of Title I is all the more true of both bilingual education and education programs for the handicapped. These programs even more explicitly call for the recruitment of specially trained staff, must be monitored by administrators with specialized qualifications, and are subject to a host of federal and state guidelines.

Federal programs have thus contributed to a broad social trend toward increasing functional specialization in American education. But what has been gained through specialization may have come at the expense of a more integrated vision of the child's educational experience. The result is what John W. Meyer calls "fragmented centralization." Confronted by a maze of distinct programs, the local administrator responsible for programs in his particular area has no choice but to:

> . . . have a differentiated subunit for each funding . . . program, let the subunits report as best they can in conformity with requirements, avoid having the subunits brought in contact with each other (so as to avoid explicit conflict or inconsistency), and remain in ignorance of the exact content of the various programs, reports, and budgets (so as to maintain a posture of incompetence, rather than dishonesty). The ideal administrator, in this sit-

uation, will be a picture of ineptitude: ignorant of the most obvious aspects of the reality nominally under supervision, and tolerant of the most egregious mistakes.[24]

Reagan administration officials have made much the same point, though in less sympathetic terms: "One lesson is clear from the past: the only real losers in converting categorical grants to a block grant are the bureaucratic middlemen—the grantsmen—who use up funds for the needy.[25]

It is incorrect to credit (or blame) the federal government exclusively for trends that are rooted broadly in society's overall inclination toward increasing specialization. But one of the most compelling criticisms of categorical programs is their potential for undermining the authority of territorially based administrators, such as school principals, and their contribution to further fragmentation of educational programs.

Categorical programs have so magnified the school's concern for the disadvantaged that mainline programs serving middle-class pupils have deteriorated. In Myron Atkin's words:

> We are seeing the establishment of . . . nonsectarian, privately supported schools . . . by middle-class parents, black and white, who have begun to see the public schools as progressively less attentive to the needs of their own children, because the schools are required to respond to the demands of various special-interest groups and the minimum competency requirements without benefit of new resources. As a result of legislative directive, handicapped children increasingly are placed in regular classrooms, without additional resources provided for the teacher, forcing the teacher to redirect attention from "average" youngsters to the new group. As another example, judges frequently send delinquent children back to classrooms from which they had been excluded because they are extraordinarily disruptive. The courts act to protect the civil rights of the excluded children. But when many of these youngsters go back to the classroom, they continue to disrupt the regular educational activities and command disproportionate amounts of teacher time. There is little doubt that many of the new schools established by middle-class parents are a response to such developments.[26]

Certain facts are quite consistent with the claim that middle-class students are at a disadvantage in the public-school system. As discussed earlier, the federal government has concentrated much of its resources on serving the educational needs of the disadvantaged, whether they be handicapped, non-English-speaking, or from low-income families. Also, middle-class students, especially in high school, are doing less well than they used to on a variety of educational achievement tests. Further, as shown in chapter 2, a higher percentage of students is now attending nonpublic schools.

But while these trends are evident, it is difficult to establish a causal link between them and federal policy. It may be that federal policies, by encouraging administrators to focus on procedural compliance rather than substantive educational goals, by fostering programs with overlapping and contradictory requirements, by fragmenting educational processes, and, above all, by championing equality (perhaps at the expense of achievement), have undermined the relationship between schools and their middle-class constituency. Yet, there are good reasons to doubt that federal policy has so affected public schools. For one thing, federal funds have never exceeded 9 percent of the operating budget of the average local school district. To claim that a small fraction of school expenditures could have pervasive, systemwide effects is to claim that the tail is wagging the dog. While such dog-wagging is not inconceivable, existing institutional arrangements in American education make it unlikely. Federal monies for education are generally distributed to the states, which then disperse funds to local school districts with which state officials worked closely for decades prior to federal programming. Because federal attempts to regulate education must pass through this state filter, the local impact of federal policy is substantially attenuated.

Even if enforcement of federal regulations were maximal, it is not clear how federal programming could have such an influence over mainline educational programs. Vocational education, impact aid, and the programs growing out of NDEA are all highly permissive federal programs. Special education for the handicapped has historically been kept separate from regular education. By all accounts, moves toward mainstreaming, where they are occurring, are due more to local reconsideration of special education policies than to strong federal pressures. Bilingual education programs seldom affect middle-class pupils from nonminority backgrounds. Title I, the largest of all federal programs, may have a more pervasive effect, but Title I funds are largely focused on elementary schools, where the level of middle-class student performances has been maintained. The considerably faster deterioration of pupil performances at the secondary-school level suggests that declining educational standards are not related to the federal role.

The Case for Existing Categorical Grants

Defenders of existing categorical programs claim that they promote national, social, and educational objectives not well served under an earlier system of state and local financing and control. They believe that "local units are not very good instruments of reform"[27] and suspect that going " 'back to local government' is in reality a call to return to control by those large corporate, union, professional, and other collections of capital and expertise which have led to many of the very problems with which the federal government now has to deal."[28] More specifically, those favoring categoricals argue that they are necessary because (1) educational programs for the disadvantaged are beyond the financial means of state and local governments; (2) block-grant monies will be taken away from programs for those with special needs and applied to more general education purposes; and (3) changing the criteria for distributing educational grants-in-aid will divert monies away from school systems presently in the greatest financial trouble.

Educational programs for the disadvantaged are beyond the financial means of state and local governments. The newest, largest, and most regulated federal education programs concentrate on the needs of low-income, handicapped, non-English-speaking, and other disadvantaged groups. Often promulgated in response to federal court decisions, they have encouraged new directions for school policy, rectifying inequalities in educational opportunity. Special services for the handicapped have been enlarged, the educational needs of the poor are explicitly being attended to, school desegregation has been hastened, and, for the first time since World War I, bilingual instruction is available. None of these advances would have been possible without the growing federal role in education. As Larry Cuban, former superintendent of schools in Arlington, Virginia, observed, "The beneficial side of state and federal influence is when intervention plainly deals with equity and opportunity. There is little doubt in my mind, for example, that without P.L. 94–142 few local school boards would have devoted resources, designed due process procedures, and improved programs and facilities for handicapped children."[29]

Others argue that while categorical programs may have been necessary to introduce these innovations, they have outlived their purpose. Two decades ago, minorities may not have been well enough organized at state and local levels to obtain the educational programs they believed were needed. But the categorical grant programs, together with such federal programs as the war on poverty, have increased the level of political organization and sophistication among low-income groups so much that these groups are no longer in need of federal protection. For example, federal regulations require that Title I, vocational education, and bilingual education programs all have local advisory councils, and these councils have become staunch defenders of these programs in many local communities. In addition, the school system contains educational specialists who have a vested interest in maintaining certain educational programs. Where categorical programs make a valuable educational contribution, they can be expected to be maintained within a block-grant funding structure.

As persuasive as this argument may be in terms of bigger cities with politically effective, large minority-group populations, the political power of disadvantaged groups varies from one local school district to another. Also, even under political conditions that favor allocating resources to the disadvantaged, local school systems must consider the serious economic costs of concentrating resources on low-income groups. As a community spends more on services for the poor and needy, it imposes a heavier tax on its more productive members, thereby discouraging their continued commitment to the area. To a much greater degree than the federal government, local governments are at the mercy of broad economic forces over which they have little or no control; if economic trends become too unfavorable, they can even go bankrupt, a condition that is becoming an increasing urban concern.

With such limited fiscal capacities, local governments have traditionally accepted only very limited social responsibilities for the poor and needy. Some welfare provision has traditionally been a "county" function, but that assistance has generally been meager. The expansion of the welfare state that began with the New Deal shifted financial responsibility markedly to the federal government. By the mid-1970s, over 70 percent of the funds supporting the major government welfare programs—including housing, medical care, food stamps, and direct cash payments—came from the federal government. The local contribution was less than 8 percent, 3 percent less than it had been two decades earlier.[30]

The assumption of the financial obligation for welfare assistance by the federal government seems entirely appropriate. If local governments were to take primary responsibility for financing welfare assistance programs, they would be poorly and unevenly funded. Communities offering the most generous support, though havens for the poor, would be forced to levy higher local taxes, thereby discouraging business investment within their boundaries. Ironically, the more a city provides for the poor, the poorer it tends to become. To some extent, such has been the fate of New York City, one of the few local governments that at one time thought it could sustain a wide variety of social services for low-income groups. But even New York, once the richest city in the world, discovered that it could not with impunity assume responsibilities that properly belonged to higher levels of government.

Although most local governments have wisely abstained from

assuming major fiscal responsibilities, education is one area that has generally been funded through local resources. While in recent years, public schools have received increasing state and federal support, 45 percent of their educational services are still financed out of local sources. This is due partly to the fact that schools are not "charity" institutions in the same way that food stamp and public housing programs are. Public schools, like police and fire departments, provide services to all social classes. Local taxpayers are thus willing and able to assume a substantial part of the fiscal burden, and businesses do not leave a local jurisdiction because of the school tax, as long as their employees' children are receiving a good education in return and the tax burden is not excessive.

But educating the children of nonproductive members of a community is costly to the local economy. Educational services for the poor and disadvantaged impose taxes on productive community members without providing benefits. Businesses and prosperous residents have every incentive to leave a community where the tax burden for educating children of poor, disadvantaged residents is high. For this reason, programs for the disadvantaged are especially difficult to finance locally.

The federal government cannot be profligate with its tax dollars either. Excessive expenditures for welfare and other social services may weaken the productive capacities of the nation as a whole, undermining its position in international competition. But the federal government can exert controls that are beyond the powers of state and local governments. For one thing, the federal government can limit immigration of low-income people from other parts of the world. It can also manipulate tariffs, product quotas, and overseas investment policies in ways that soften the domestic impact of worldwide economic changes. Moreover, the federal government can command the loyalty of its citizens and businesses in ways that Newark, New Jersey, and Boise, Idaho, cannot. To leave the country for tax purposes is quite different from moving to New Hampshire from Massachusetts. Thus, the federal government has a greater capacity to finance programs for the needy and poor than do state and local governments.

Blocks-grant monies will be taken away from those with special needs and applied to more general education programs. When a block grant is given to states and localities, the monies are likely to be incorporated in the regular budgets of the schools and spent on purposes indistinguishable from those supported by local monies. Such a diversion of funds from special programs is especially likely to occur if the block grant is instituted at a time when aid is substantially reduced and/or when local school districts are facing serious budgetary deficiencies. Both the greater political strength of middle-class constituents and the urgency for using tax dollars for services desired by productive community members can be expected to press local school officials to greatly reduce or even eliminate categorical programs. According to Norman Chockin of the Lawyers Committee for Civil Rights under Law, "Given the extent of the need, in many school districts there may be no funds left over for other programs, especially in light of the budget reductions and inflation rates."[31]

These expectations are supported by experience with the general revenue-sharing program passed by Congress in 1973. Robert Shapiro's careful study of the way in which these funds were spent by local governments found that "general revenue sharing [and] community development block grants . . . tend to substitute for locally raised expenditure funds, while . . . categorical forms of assistance tend to stimulate local expeditures."[32] Research currently under way at Stanford, under the direction of Henry M. Levin, also indicates that whereas federal categorical grants in education do not reduce local contributions, general state aid (a block-grant allocation) is often used by school districts as a substitute for local financing.[33] In other words, when the constraints on local government use of federal funds are lifted, recent experiences suggest that these monies are as likely to be used for tax relief as for extending local services. If this is the goal of federal education policy, a move toward the block-grant approach seems appropriate. But critics fear that the education of disadvantaged groups would suffer the most as federal dollars become available for other purposes.

Changing the criteria for distributing educational grants-in-aid will divert monies away from those school systems presently in the greatest financial trouble. When political leaders take stands on grants-in-aid programs, their positions are influenced not only by the effects of the program on various social groups but also by its geographical impact. As shown in chapter 4, Democratic support for Title I was due in part to the disproportionate level of expenditures earmarked for big cities and for rural areas of the (then) Democratic South. Urban congressmen have regularly fought the rural bias of vocational education funding to secure more monies for urban areas. In the case of aid to federally impacted school districts, the definition of "federal impact" on local school districts has been continuously broadened so that nearly every congressional district has a community within it that is in one way or another eligible for funding. Even though the Emergency School Aid Act (ESAA) was supposed to help school districts undergoing desegregation, the guideline for allocation of funds was based on the number of minority students living within a state, a guideline that increased the number of eligible school districts but shifted funding away from the South, which at the time the program passed was the area of the country desegregating most rapidly. Support for and opposition to block-grant proposals are also likely to be influenced by calculations of their geographical impact. It is widely anticipated that the Reagan administration block-grant funding formulas will shift funds away from the large urban areas of the Northeast and Midwest (primary beneficiaries of Title I funding) to middle-sized cities and suburban areas throughout the country.

The general revenue-sharing legislation passed during the Nixon administration had exactly these effects. Unlike the categorical grants, which favored large central cities, the formula for distributing monies under revenue sharing gave roughly equal weight to size of population, general tax effort, and relative income. Thus many governments in smaller and more rural parts of the United States began receiving federal monies for the first time. The amount per capita received by local government in major metropolitan areas was somewhat less than the average per capita amount distributed nationwide.[34] On the other hand, the twenty-five largest cities received more federal revenue-sharing funds per capita than did their surrounding suburbs.[35]

If the formula for distributing educational grants-in-aid were to take a similar form, funding would probably shift from large cities in the Northeast and Midwest, which have received disproportionate amounts under categorical grants, to middle-sized cities, suburbs, and smaller towns, and to the West. While such a shift in funding would correspond well with the Reagan administration's political base of support, replacement of categoricals with this kind of block grant will aggravate the fiscal problems of declining economic regions and reinforce an already pronounced population shift to the South and West.

The fiscal impact of a block-grant program on central cities could be especially severe. At a time when federal funds for education are being cut 25 to 35 percent, a shift in the formula for distributing federal dollars might leave big cities with less than half the federal dollars in 1983 than they received in 1981. In a situation already financially precarious, a sharp change in federal policy might push a number of school districts toward bankruptcy.

Nothing in the concept of block grants compels such a result; if a formula for distributing monies for education is based on the number of low-income, handicapped, and otherwise disadvantaged children, geographical shifts in funding would be less marked. But if the basis for distributing funds is the number of disadvantaged pupils in a school district, then the block grant becomes a categorical program.

Conclusions

The crisis in American education is greatly exaggerated. For decades the American educational system has flourished: public-school enrollment expanded, pupil-teacher ratios were reduced, teachers' salaries increased, the curriculum became diversified, and taxpayers provided a steadily growing share of the gross national product for education. Schools were valued as one of the few public institutions that were part of every community, that reached all classes and races, that combined a sensitivity to regional and local differences with a capacity to provide a relatively standard set of services, and that symbolized the nation's democratic ideal of equal opportunity and citizen responsibility.

But even though American schools remain fundamentally sound—elementary-school children are learning how to read as well as they ever have, and the differences in academic performance between the races are noticeably narrowing—several problems have arisen. As the number of young Americans declined in the 1970s and 1980s, the employment opportunities for educators have been sharply reduced, teachers' salaries have fallen, the percentage of the nation's resources allocated to education has passed its peak, and per pupil expenditures have reached a plateau. At the same time, the public's confidence in its public schools has deteriorated, the percentage of children in private schools has begun to climb, and the academic performances of high-school students have waned, especially in mathematics and science. After so many decades of steady expansion and improvement, these signs of stabilization and even decline have generated calls for reappraisal and renewal.

Those who have identified the federal government as the chief cause of current discontent are mistaken. It is true that since 1965 the federal government's role in education has been more extensive, more program-oriented, more attentive to questions of equal opportunity, and more demanding in terms of regulation than it traditionally had been. But this upsurge in federal control can hardly account for the sense of malaise that took hold in the late 1970s and early 1980s. In the first place, signs of decline are most noticeable in the high schools, while the largest, and one of the most intrusive, federal programs—compensatory education—generally focused on the elementary school. Second, slipping academic performance is more pronounced among students from white and middle-class families, while most federal programs have addressed the needs of the minorities, the educationally disadvantaged, and the handicapped. Third, federal programs have usually supplemented, not supplanted, programmatic offerings of local schools. While this may at times be inefficient, it is unlikely to be responsible for educational decline.

Undoubtedly, school desegregation efforts made either under court order or at the direction of the Office of Civil Rights have too often been disruptive to the education of those involved. Yet it cannot be said that nationwide school integration has been put forward with undue haste. According to one account, the degree of segregation in public schools was greater in 1980 than in 1970.[36] And it is questionable whether the nation's political well-being could have been preserved had federal pressures for racial integration been any less intense. If the price of racial harmony has been a modest diminution in the quality of education, can any thoughtful observer, taking a long-term perspective, doubt that the benefit is worth the cost?

To spare the federal government from charges that it has ruined the American public school is not to exonerate its education policies altogether. As shown in earlier chapters, in their eagerness to achieve reform, federal administrators created regulations and specifications that at times substitute inferior centrally determined educational theory for sound local prudence and judgment. Prompted by federal guidelines, for example, pupils were taken out of well-functioning regular classrooms and given so-called intensive instruction by teacher aides—instruction that sometimes proved to be of less-than-certain benefit. In the name of federally mandated "mainstreaming," handicapped children have been taken from therapeutic settings to become marginal members of regular classrooms. These and other uses and abuses of federal directives have undoubtedly contributed to inappropriate student placements, poor utilization of classroom time, and excessive administrative paperwork.

Yet the complex, decentralized American educational system has remarkable recuperative powers. When federal and state compensatory education programs conflicted, Congress rewrote the law to allow for closer coordination. When the regulations governing programs for the handicapped were out of synchronization with those that applied to compensatory education programs, the Department of Education undertook a full-scale review and developed more harmonious alternatives. When proposed regulations for the bilingual education program became excessively obtrusive, the Department of Education revised them and finally withdrew them altogether. But the self-correcting capabilities of our educational system are best illustrated by the 1981 Reconciliation Act.

While the 1981 Reconciliation Act was the product of a complex bargaining process and represents neither the expressed preferences of the Reagan administration nor those of the Democratic opposition in Congress, what emerged seems to have rectified many of the deficiencies in federal education programs that existed in 1980. The National Defense Education Act (NDEA) and impact aid programs, both of which were said to lack a well-defined federal purpose, were either folded into a block grant or severely cut back in terms of budget. Congress greatly simplified the excessive regulatory detail of the compensatory education program and eliminated the Emergency School Aid program, so beset by political compromise that only rarely did it assist the process of school desegregation to any substantial degree. Unfortunately, education bore more than its share of the 1981 budget reduction, and it is hoped that in the future Congress will restore and extend the financial aid that the federal government gives to local schools. But the administrative and organizational changes made may, in the long run, prove to be both more beneficial and more significant than the budgetary changes.

While many argue that the 1981 Reconciliation Act was passed without adequate legislative deliberation, it is difficult for any detached observer to quarrel seriously with the political and program judgments made on its nonbudgetary aspects. To a large extent, the compromise combined the best elements of the block-grant concept with a continuing recognition that equal opportunity remains a principal federal objective.

The 1981 Reconciliation Act may well have found an acceptable balance between federal definition of national objectives and local determination of administrative requirements. Judgment must be reserved on this point until the law has been implemented and its full consequences become clear. Quite certainly, defects will be identified; just as surely, these problems will form the basis for new group, partisan, legislative, and administrative initiatives. Such is the process through which a balance among competing interests and concerns is generally achieved.

But if Congress has recently been moving in the right direction on administrative and organizational matters, it has yet to achieve an appropriate balance among competing objectives in its pursuit of quality education. Even in the 1980s, with conservative forces in ascendance, federal programs have still been largely confined to questions of equal access and equal opportunity. In large part, this is due to the desire to keep in place existing programs (which have an equal opportunity thrust) in the face of heavy budgetary pressures. New initiatives are not easily launched under such circumstances. As a result, federal education policy in 1982, under Reagan, was as focused on matters of equal opportunity as it had been in 1980, and much more than it had been in 1976. Compensatory education and programs for the handicapped, for example, received a significantly greater percentage of the Department of Education's elementary- and secondary-school program budget in 1982 than it did in 1976 (see Table 3–1).

Given the special role that the federal government must play in ensuring equal educational opportunity, this recent trend should not, under the circumstances, be criticized. But there is also need for an explicit expression of federal attention to issues of educational quality. By almost exclusively focusing on equal opportunity, the Department of Education has implied that educational quality is unimportant, as though, if access to schools is given equally to everyone, learning will take care of itself.

Some may feel this criticism is unfair and misleading. After all, the Department of Education has funded many studies that were expected to lead to improved classroom performances. Its almost obsessive emphasis on testing and evaluation reveals a commitment to quality education. The Department of Education also developed programs for the gifted, encouraged innovations in curriculum, and hailed the achievements of outstanding educators. But even while these projects were carried out, the focus of the Department of Education, at least since the mid-1970s, has been on questions of equal access and equal opportunity. The appointment of Shirley Hufstedler, a federal judge known for her strong civil-rights concerns, as the first head of the Department of Education, both exemplified and symbolized the department's basic commitments.

Without eschewing these concerns, the Department of Education (or any successor institution) must demonstrate its commitment to quality education. Needless to say, that goal must be pursued differently from equal opportunity programs, as described earlier, which required federal direction, regulation, and control. The pursuit of quality education requires instead very few federal controls and regulations because local school districts will not be asked to do anything other than what they very much want to do. In this case, the Department of Education must show leadership, bring the issue to national attention, and stimulate new approaches to solving the problem. While the mechanisms by which educational quality can be enhanced must be decentralized and dispersed, intelligent and resourceful national leadership can give direction to what otherwise might dissipate in the crosscurrents of routine decisionmaking.

In the early 1980s, there has been renewed attention to the issue of the quality of education from all shades of the political spectrum. In 1981, Department of Education Secretary Bell appointed a national Commission on Educational Excellence. In 1982, the Johnson Foundation sponsored a conference at Wingspread attended by some thirty-five representatives from groups and organizations undertaking major studies of the quality of education in secondary schools. In the spring of 1983, President Reagan proposed a $50 million federal program to enhance instruction in science and mathematics. At the same time, several Democratic contenders for the presidential nomination have insisted that the country maintain and upgrade both its physical and human capital. Just as Sputnik inspired concern for the quality of American education in the 1950s, so Japanese technology and vigorous competition from other foreign countries have awakened public interest in education as the means to enhance national productivity.

The educational reforms now under way will be influenced by the direction these and other national leaders provide, and such efforts are to be applauded. Yet the final results will depend on the myriad decisions and commitments made by men and women in school boards and classrooms throughout the country. Because our country both suffers from and enjoys government by decentralized institutions, there will remain, for better or worse, a gulf between the goals set by federal policy and the state of American education.

NOTES

Chapter 1

1. Arnold J. Heidenheimer, "The Politics of Public Education, Health and Welfare in the U.S. and Western Europe: How Growth and Reform Potentials Have Differed" (Paper presented at the meeting of the American Political Science Association, Washington, D.C., September 1972).

2. See chap. 2, Tables 2–9 and 2–13.

3. Carl L. Marburger, quoted in "How Should Schools Be Ruled?" *Educational Leadership* 38 (November 1980), p. 108.

4. Cynthia Parsons, "Attention: Secretary Hufstedler," *Phi Delta Kappan* (March 1980), pp. 448–49.

5. Albert Shanker, quoted in "Washington Report," *Phi Delta Kappan* (November 1980), p. 165.

6. Max Rafferty, "The Spark That Kindles," *Education* (Winter 1980), p. 106.

7. Terry Herndon, quoted in "Washington Report," *Phi Delta Kappan* (November 1980), pp. 170–71.

8. Michael W. Kirst, "Loss of Support for Public Schools: Some Causes and Solutions," *Daedalus* (Summer 1981), p. 31.

9. Albert H. Quie, quoted in "How Should Schools Be Ruled?" *Educational Leadership* 38 (November 1980), p. 108.

10. Harold Howe II, "Two Views of the New Department of Education and Its First Secretary," *Phi Delta Kappan* (March 1980), p. 447.

11. Anne Campbell, as quoted in "How Should Schools Be Ruled?" *Educational Leadership* 38 (November 1980), p. 103.

12. David Savage, "Education of a New Department," *Educational Leadership* 38 (November 1980), p. 117.

13. J. Myron Atkin, "The Government in the Classroom," *Daedalus* 109 (Summer 1980), pp. 85–97.

14. Albert Shanker, quoted in "How Should Schools Be Ruled?" *Educational Leadership* 38 (November 1980), p. 105.

15. Joseph M. Cronin, "The Federal Takeover: Should the Junior Partner Run the Firm?" *Federalism at the Crossroads: Improving Educational Policymaking* (Washington, D.C.: Institute for Educational Leadership, 1976), p. 2.

16. Ronald Reagan, quoted in "Reagan Urges 3Rs+P," *Chicago Tribune,* March 13, 1983.

17. U.S. Office of Management and Budget, *Fiscal Year 1982 Budget Revisions* (Washington, D.C.: U.S. Government Printing Office, 1976), p. 136.

18. Harrison Donnelly, "Scaled-Down Block Grants Near Enactment," *Congressional Quarterly Weekly Report,* July 4, 1981, p. 1180.

Chapter 2

1. James A. Sweet and Linda Jacobsen, "A Demographic Look at the Supply and Demand for Teachers" (Paper prepared for the Conference on Teachers and Policy, National Institute of Education, Washington, D.C., February 1981).

2. Ibid.

3. Michael W. Kirst, "Loss of Support for Public Schools: Some Causes and Solutions," *Daedalus* (Summer 1981).

4. James S. Coleman, *Equality of Educational Opportunity,* report prepared for the U.S. Department of Education (Washington, D.C.: National Center for Education Statistics, 1966).

5. The results for the science tests are given in Department of Education, National Center for Education Statistics, *Digest of Educational Statistics* (Washington, D.C.: U.S. Government Printing Office, 1980, 1982 eds.).

Chapter 3

1. Frank J. Munger and Richard F. Fenno, Jr., *National Politics and Federal Aid to Education* (Syracuse, N.Y.: Syracuse University Press, 1962), p. 28.

2. Ibid., chap. 4.

3. Ibid., p. 98.

4. National Institute of Education, "Federal Vocational Education

Legislation," *The Vocational Education Study: The Interim Report* (Washington, D.C.: U.S. Department of Education, 1980), p. II–3.

5. Marvin Lazerson and W. Norton Grubb, eds., *American Education and Vocationalism: A Documentary History, 1870–1970* (New York: Teachers College Press, Columbia University, 1974), p. 28.

6. National Institute of Education, "Federal Vocational Education Legislation," pp. II–3, 8.

7. Munger and Fenno, *National Politics and Federal Aid to Education,* p. 100.

8. Ibid., p. 50.

9. Stephen K. Bailey, *Education Interest Groups in the Nation's Capital* (Washington, D.C.: American Council on Education, 1975), p. 28.

10. Harry L. Summerfield, *Power and Process: The Formulation and Limits of Federal Educational Policy* (Berkeley, Calif.: McCutchan, 1974), p. 25.

11. *Vocational Education Act, Statutes at Large* 77, sec. 1, 403 (1963).

12. Ibid., sec. 3.

13. Summerfield, *Power and Process,* p. 10.

14. Federal expenditures for vocational education increased from $416.9 million in 1972 to $823.7 million by 1983. See Table 3–1.

15. Joel S. Berke and Michael W. Kirst, *Federal Aid to Education: Who Benefits? Who Governs?* (Lexington, Mass.: D.C. Heath, 1972), p. 259.

16. Charles Benson and E. Gareth Hoachlander, "Descriptive Study of the Distribution of Federal, State and Local Funds for Vocational Education" (Final report of the Project on Vocational Education Resources, Berkeley, University of California School of Education, September 1981). See also Paul E. Peterson and Barry G. Rabe, "Career Training or Education for Life: Dilemmas in the Development of Chicago Vocational Education" (Paper prepared for the National Institute of Education, Washington, D.C., March 1981).

17. *Education Amendments of 1976, Statutes at Large* 90, sec. 107, 2180 (1976).

18. Paul E. Peterson and Barry G. Rabe, "Urban Vocational Education and Managing the Transition from School to Work" (Paper prepared for the National Institute of Education, Washington, D.C., March 1981), pp. 32–33.

19. Legislative Analyst, *Vocational Education in California* (Sacramento: State of California, April 1977), p. 14.

20. Abt Associates, "Implementation of the Education Amendments

of 1976: A Study of State and Local Compliance and Evaluation Practices in Vocational Education" (Washington, D.C.: National Institute
of Education, 1980), p. 53.

21. *Education Amendments of 1976, Statutes at Large* 90, sec. 112,
2187 (1976).

22. Peterson and Rabe, "Urban Vocational Education and Managing the Transition from School to Work," p. 34.

23. Abt Associates, "Implementation of the Education Amendments
of 1976," p. 97.

24. *Education Amendments of 1976, Statutes at Large* 90, sec. 101,
2169 (1976).

25. Peterson and Rabe, "Urban Vocational Education and Managing the Transition from School to Work," p. 36.

26. *Education Amendments of 1976, Statutes at Large* 90, sec. 105,
2176 (1976).

27. Peterson and Rabe, "Urban Vocational Education and Managing the Transition from School to Work," pp. 36–37.

28. *National Defense Education Act of 1958, Statutes at Large* 72,
sec. 301, 1588 (1958).

29. Sidney Sufrin, *Administering the National Defense Education Act*
(Syracuse, N.Y.: Syracuse University Press, 1963), p. 13.

30. Executive Committee of American Association of School
Administrators, as quoted in "Editorial," *The Nation's Schools* 67
(February 1961), pp. 61–62.

31. "Federal Aid: Don't Let It Unbalance the Curriculum," *The
Nation's Schools* 66 (November 1960), p. 77.

32. U.S. Department of Health, Education, and Welfare, Office of
Education, *Guide to the National Defense Education Act* (Washington,
D.C.: U.S. Government Printing Office, 1959), p. 9.

33. Sufrin, *Administering the National Defense Education Act,* p.
31.

34. Paul Marsh and Ross Gortner, *Federal Aid to Science Education:
Two Programs* (Syracuse, N.Y.: Syracuse University Press, 1963), p.
41.

35. Lorraine McDonnell et al., *Program Consolidation and the State
Role in ESEA Title IV,* report prepared for the U.S. Office of Educa-
tion, Department of Health, Education, and Welfare (Santa Monica,
Calif.: Rand Corp., 1980).

36. Robert Procumier, "The Impact of Title III, NDEA on Programs
in the Public Schools of Illinois" (Ed.D. diss., Indiana University,
Bloomington, 1962).

37. U.S. Department of Health, Education, and Welfare, Office of

Education, *NDEA Title III, Fiscal Years 1959–1967: A Management View* (Washington, D.C.: U.S. Government Printing Office, 1969), p. 17.

38. U.S. Department of Health, Education, and Welfare, Office of Education, *Strengthening Instruction in Academic Subjects, NDEA Annual Report, Fiscal Year 1972* (Washington, D.C.: U.S. Government Printing Office, 1974), p. 6.

39. Ibid., p. 9.

40. Ibid., p. 11.

41. U.S. Department of Health, Education, and Welfare, Office of Education, *NDEA Title III, Fiscal Years 1959–67*, p. 6.

42. McDonnell et al., *Program Consolidation.*

43. I. T. Johnson, "An Evaluation of NDEA Title III," *Phi Delta Kappan* 48 (June 1967), p. 500.

44. McDonnell et al., *Program Consolidation*, p. 12.

45. Ibid., p. 15.

46. *Congressional Quarterly Almanac* (Washington, D.C.: Congressional Quarterly, 1961), p. 243.

47. U.S. Office of Education, "Administration of Public Laws 81–874 and 81–815," *Annual Report of the Commissioner of Education, Fiscal Year 1978* (Washington, D.C.: U.S. Government Printing Office, 1978), p. 23.

48. I. M. Labovitz, *Aid for Federally Affected Public Schools* (Syracuse, N.Y.: Syracuse University Press, 1963), p. 45.

49. U.S. Congress, House Committee on Education and Labor, *Impact Aid, Hearings before a Subcommittee of the House Committee on Education and Labor*, 95th Cong., 1st sess., 1977, pp. 801–02.

50. Ibid., p. 887.

51. Ibid., pp. 12, 29.

Chapter 4

1. *Elementary and Secondary Education Act of 1965, Statutes at Large* 79, sec. 27 (1965).

2. National Institute of Education, *Title I Funds Allocation: The Current Formula* (Washington, D.C.: U.S. Department of Health, Education, and Welfare, 1977).

3. *Congressional Quarterly Weekly Report*, December 28, 1974, p. 3423.

4. Ibid., March 16, 1974, p. 701.

5. Ibid.

6. Michale Timpane, ed., *The Federal Interest in Financing Schooling* (Cambridge, Mass.: Ballinger, 1978), p. xxiii.

7. Michael O. Reagan and John G. Sanzone, *The New Federalism* (New York: Oxford University Press, 1981), p. 114.

8. U.S. Congress, House Committee on Education and Labor, *Hearings before a Subcommittee of the House Committee on Education and Labor on "Elementary and Secondary Education Amendments of 1973,"* 93rd Cong, 1st sess., 1973, p. 847.

9. Ibid., p. 847.

10. Paul Hill, *Compensatory Education Services*, report prepared for the U.S. Department of Education (Washington, D.C.: National Institute of Education, July 1977).

11. *Elementary and Secondary Education Act of 1965, Statutes at Large* 79, sec. 604 (1965).

12. Ibid., sec. 205, 5.

13. Jane L. David, *Local Uses of Title I Evaluations* (Menlo Park, Calif.: Stanford Research Institute, 1978), p. 3.

14. Michael W. Kirst and Richard Jung, "The Utility of a Longitudinal Approach in Assessing Implementation: A Thirteen Year View of Title I ESEA," *Educational Evaluation and Policy Analysis* 2 (1980), p. 25.

15. Jerome T. Murphy, "Title I of ESEA: The Politics of Implementing Federal Education Reform," *Harvard Educational Review* 41 (February 1971), p. 43.

16. Ibid., pp. 46–47.

17. Kirst and Jung, "The Utility of a Longitudinal Approach in Assessing Implementation," p. 26.

18. Murphy, "Title I of ESEA," p. 42.

19. Washington Research Project of the Southern Center for Studies in Public Policy and the NAACP Legal Defense and Educational Fund, *Title I of ESEA, Is It Helping Poor Children?* (1969), as cited in Murphy, "Title I of ESEA," p. 44.

20. Robert Goettel, "Financing Assistance to National Target Groups: The ESEA Title I Experience," in *The Federal Interest in Financing Schooling,* ed. Michael Timpane (Cambridge, Mass.: Ballinger, 1978), p. 184.

21. Stanford Research Institute, *Research on the Effectiveness of Compensatory Education Programs* (Menlo Park, Calif.: 1977), p. iii.

22. National Institute of Education, *Administration of Compensatory Education* (Washington, D.C.: U.S. Department of Health, Education, and Welfare, 1977), p. 40.

23. Ibid., p. 44.

24. Ibid., p. 39; Elizabeth R. Reisner, *The Office of Education*

Administers Changes in a Law: Agency Response to Title I, ESEA Amendments of 1978 (Washington, D.C.: NTS Research Corporation, 1980).

25. Milbrey McLaughlin, *Evaluation and Reform: The Elementary and Secondary Education Act of 1965, Title I* (Cambridge, Mass: Ballinger, 1975), p. 2.

26. Ibid., p. 23.

27. Robert E. Barnes and Alan L. Ginsburg, "Relevance of the RMC Models for Title I Policy Concerns," *Educational Evaluation and Policy Analysis* 1 (1979), p. 7.

28. David, *Local Uses of Title I Evaluations,* p. 13.

29. Ibid., p. 16.

30. Ibid., p. 17.

31. R. J. Rossi et al., *Summaries of Major Title I Evaluations 1966–1976* (Palo Alto, Calif.: American Institutes for Research, 1977), p. 134.

32. Ibid., p. 142.

33. Ibid., p. 114.

34. Ibid., pp. 108–10.

35. M. Wang, "Evaluating the Effectiveness of Compensatory Education" (Paper presented at the annual meeting of the American Educational Research Association, Boston, 1980), p. 3, as cited in William W. Cooley, "Effectiveness of Compensatory Education," *Educational Leadership* (January 1981), p. 300.

36. Ibid.

37. U.S. Congress, House Committee on Education and Labor, *Hearings before a Subcommittee of the House Committee on Education and Labor on the "Elementary and Secondary Education Amendments of 1973,"* 93rd Cong., 1st sess., 1973, p. 419.

38. Ibid., p. 386.

39. J. Meyer, "Organizational Factors Affecting Legalization in Education" (Paper presented to the IFG Seminar on Law and Governance in Education, Stanford, Calif., October 1980), p. 25.

40. William W. Cooley and Gaea Leinhardt, "The Instructional Dimensions Study," *Educational Evaluation and Policy Analysis* 2 (1980), pp. 7–25.

41. Wang, "Evaluating the Effectiveness of Compensatory Education," p. 8, as cited in Cooley, "Effectiveness of Compensatory Education," p. 300.

42. G. V. Glass and M. L. Smith, " 'Pull Out' in Compensatory Education" (Boulder, Colo.: Laboratory of Educational Research, University of Colorado, 1977), as cited in Cooley, "Effectiveness of Compensatory Education," p. 300.

43. For example, J. Epstein examined data from a national sample of ninety-four elementary schools and found that:

> . . . after the bus stops at the desegregated school, resegregation occurs in the classroom. Over half of the teachers track students into classrooms by ability; over 80 percent regroup the children by ability within the class. Only 25 percent report track assignments flexible enough to permit 20 percent of the students to change tracks from the time they enter to the time they leave the school.

In Epstein, "After the Bus Arrives: Resegregation in Desegrated Schools" (Paper presented at the annual meeting of the American Educational Research Association, Boston, April 7–12, 1980), as cited by Willis D. Hawley, "Increasing the Effectiveness of School Desegregation: Lessons from the Research" (Durham, N.C.: Duke University Center for Educational Policy, Institute of Policy Sciences and Policy Affairs, July 1980).

Chapter 5

1. Susan Gilbert Schneider, *Revolution, Reaction or Reform* (New York: Las Americas, 1977), p. 7.
2. Ibid., p. 28.
3. Ibid., p. 142.
4. U.S. Office of Education, *Annual Evaluation Report on Programs Administered by the U.S. Office of Education, Fiscal Year 1979* (Washington, D.C.: U.S. Department of Education, 1980), pp. 198–99.
5. U.S. Office of Education, *Condition of Education for Hispanic Americans* (Washington, D.C.: National Center for Education Statistics, July 1980), p. 26.
6. "Evaluation of the Impact of ESEA Title VII Spanish/English Bilingual Education Program: Abstract and Summary of Findings," *Bilingual Resources* 1 (Winter 1978), p. 2.
7. Lutz Erbring, "High School and Beyond Summary Report: An Overview of Outcomes in Secondary Education" (Mimeograph, National Opinion Research Center, Chicago, 1980), pp. 12–13.
8. Noel Epstein, *Language, Ethnicity, and the Schools: Policy Alternatives for Bilingual-Bicultural Education* (Washington, D.C.: Institute for Educational Leadership, 1977), p. 4.
9. Ibid., p. 88.
10. U.S. President, *Weekly Compilation of Presidential Documents*

(Washington, D.C.: Office of the *Federal Register,* National Archives and Records Service, 1953–   ), Gerald R. Ford, December 8, 1975, p. 1335.

11. *The Education for All Handicapped Children Act of 1975, Statutes at Large* 89, sec. 3–b, 773–796 (1975).

12. Frederick J. Weintraub, ed., *Public Policy and the Education of Exceptional Children* (Washington, D.C.: Council for Exceptional Children, 1976), p. 9.

13. Ibid.

14. U.S. Office of Education, *Progress Toward a Free Appropriate Public Education* (Washington, D.C.: U.S. Department of Health, Education, and Welfare, 1979), p. 17.

15. Ibid., p. 113.

16. Anne W. Wright, *Local Implementation of P.L. 94–142: Second Year Report of a Longitudinal Study* (Menlo Park, Calif.: Stanford Research Institute, 1980), p. 105.

17. Ibid., p. 109.

18. Ibid., p. 112.

19. Michael W. Kirst and Kay A. Bertken, "Due Process Hearings in Special Education: An Exploration of Who Benefits" (Mimeograph, National Institute of Education, Washington, D.C., 1980).

20. U.S. Congress, House Committee on Education and Labor, Hearing before a Subcommittee of the Committee on Education and Labor, *Oversight of Public Law 94–142, The Education for All Handicapped Children Act,* 96th Cong., 1st sess., March 1979, p. 82.

21. Wright, *Local Implementation of P.L. 94–142,* p. 101; Richard Weatherly and Michael Lipsky, "Street-Level Bureaucrats and Institutional Innovation: Implementing Special Education Reform," *Harvard Educational Review* 47 (May 1977), pp. 171–97.

22. U.S. Congress, House Subcommittee on Education, *Oversight of Public Law 94–142,* p. 233.

23. *Congressional Quarterly Weekly Report,* May 29, 1970, p. 1164.

24. Ibid.

25. Gary Orfield, *Must We Bus?* (Washington, D.C.: Brookings Institution, 1978), p. 246.

26. *Congressional Quarterly Weekly Report,* June 19, 1970, p. 1585.

27. Ibid.

28. Ibid., December 11, 1970, p. 2946.

29. Ibid., February 9, 1974, pp. 267-68.

30. Ibid.

31. Stephen M. Smith, *An Assessment of Emergency School Aid Act Program Operations: The Targetting of ESAA Grants and Grant Funds* (Washington, D.C.: Applied Urbanetics, 1978), p. 2.

32. Ibid.

33. Anne H. MacQueen and John E. Coulson, *Emergency School Aid Act Evaluations: Overview of Findings from Supplemental Analyses* (Santa Monica, Calif.: System Development Corp., 1978), p. 9.

34. Orfield, *Must We Bus?* p. 246.

Chapter 6

1. California State Board of Education, "Summary of Evidence of the Decline in Academic Programs in California Schools" (Mimeograph, 1981).

2. Chris Pipho, "Competency Testing: A Response to Arthur Wise," *Educational Leadership* (May 1979), p. 551.

3. Ibid., p. 552.

4. William G. Spady, "The Concept and Implications of Competency-Based Education," *Educational Leadership* (October 1978), p. 16.

5. Lutz Erbring, "High School and Beyond Summary Report: An Overview of Outcomes in Secondary Education" (Mimeograph, National Opinion Research Center, Chicago, 1980), p. 44.

6. Arthur Wise, *Legislated Learning: The Bureaucratization of the American Classroom* (Berkeley: University of California Press, 1979), pp. 60–61.

7. James Coleman, Thomas Hoffer, and Sally Kilgore, *Public and Private Schools* (Chicago: National Opinion Research Center, 1981).

8. Arthur S. Goldberger, "Coleman Goes Private (In Public)" (Mimeograph, Stanford Center for Advanced Study in the Behavioral Sciences, Stanford University, 1981); Richard J. Murname, "Evidence, Analysis, and Unanswered Questions: Coleman's New Study, *Public and Private Schools*" (Mimeograph, Yale University, New Haven, 1981).

9. Coleman, Hoffer, and Kilgore, *Public and Private Schools,* p. 120.

10. Ibid., p. 70.

11. James Catterall, "Tuition Credits for Schools: A Federal Priority for the 1980s" (Policy paper, Institute for Research on Educational Finance and Governance, Stanford University, Stanford, Calif., 1981).

12. "Tax Credits Unlikely to Benefit Low-Income Families, CBO Says," *Education Daily,* February 27, 1981, p. 2.

13. Gary Orfield, ed., "Symposium on School Desegregation and

White Flight" (Center for National Policy Review, Washington, D.C., 1975).

14. Gary Orfield, *Must We Bus?* (Washington, D.C.: Brookings Institution, 1978).

15. W. E. Oates, "The Effects of Property Taxes and Local Public Spending on Property Values: An Empirical Study of Tax Capitalization and the Tiebout Hypothesis," *Journal of Political Economy* 77 (1969), pp. 957–71; H. S. Rosen and D. J. Fullerton, "A Note on Local Tax Rates, Public Benefit Levels and Property Values," *Journal of Political Economy* 85 (1977), pp. 433–40; G. R. Meadows, "Taxes, Spending, and Property Values: A Comment and Further Results," *Journal of Political Economy* 84 (1976), pp. 869–74; G. S. McDougall, "Local Public Goods and Residential Property Values: Some Insights and Extensions," *National Tax Journal* 20 (1976), pp. 436–47; Paul E. Peterson and Susan Sherman Karpluss, "The Impact of Property Taxes and Educational Expenditures on Property Values in Central Cities and Suburban Communities" (Mimeograph, Department of Political Science, University of Chicago, Chicago, 1978).

16. Rochelle L. Stanford, "The Public School Lobby Fends Off Tuition Tax Credits—At Least for Now," *National Journal,* June 13, 1981, p. 1064.

17. Heritage Foundation, "Project Team Report for the Department of Education" (Unpublished Mandate for Leadership Paper, Washington, D.C., October 29, 1980), p. 55.

18. Institute for Research on Educational Finance and Governance, "Categorical Grants in Education: Rethinking the Federal Role" (Stanford, Calif.: Institute for Research on Educational Finance and Governance, Spring 1981), p. 3.

19. Wise, *Legislated Learning,* p. 192.

20. R. E. Callahan, *Education and the Cult of Efficiency* (Chicago: University of Chicago Press, 1962); M. B. Katz, *The Irony of Early School Reform: Educational Innovation in Mid-Nineteenth Century Massachusetts* (Cambridge, Mass.: Harvard University Press, 1968); and M. B. Katz, *Class, Bureaucracy, and Schools: The Illusion of Educational Change in America* (New York: Praeger, 1971).

21. Wise, *Legislated Learning,* chap. 4.

22. Personal conversation with Russ Vlaanderen, Education Commission of the States, Denver, Colo. (July 1981).

23. Alan L. Ginsburg, Marshall S. Smith, and Brenda J. Turnbull, "Directions for Federal Elementary/Secondary Education Policy" (Mimeograph, University of Wisconsin School of Education, Madison, October 1980), pp. 5–6.

24. John W. Meyer, "The Impact of the Centralization of Education-

al Funding and Control on State and Local Organizational Governance" (Stanford, Calif.: Institute for Research on Educational Finance and Governance, August 1979), p. 17.

25. Institute for Research on Education Finance and Governance, "Categorical Grants in Education," p. 3.

26. J. Myron Atkin, "The Government in the Classroom," *Daedalus* (Summer 1980), p. 94.

27. Frederick M. Wirt, "Neoconservatism and National School Policy," *Educational Evaluation and Policy Analysis* 2 (November-December 1980), p. 14.

28. Ibid.

29. Larry Cuban, "How Should Schools Be Ruled?" *Educational Leadership* 38 (November 1980), p. 109.

30. Paul E. Peterson, *City Limits* (Chicago: University of Chicago Press, 1981), p. 80.

31. Norman Chockin, quoted in "Block Grants: Civil Rights Threat of Educational Streamlining?" *Education Daily,* March 11, 1981, p. 2.

32. Robert Shapiro, "Federal Grants and Local Expenditure" (Mimeograph, Department of Political Science, University of Chicago, 1980), p. 24. Other research has yielded similar results. For examples, see Edward M. Gramlich and George L. Perry, eds., *Brookings Papers on Economic Activity* (Washington, D.C.: Brookings Institution, 1973); Edward M. Gramlich, "Intergovernmental Grants: A Review of the Empirical Literature," in *The Political Economy of Fiscal Federalism,* ed. Wallace E. Oates (Lexington, Mass.: Lexington Books, 1977), pp. 219–37; Advisory Commission on Intergovernmental Relations, *Federal Grants: Their Effects on State-Local Expenditures, Employment Levels, and Wage Rates* (Washington, D.C.: ACIR, 1977), pp. 64–65.

33. Another study of Title I expenditures has shown that approximately two-thirds of Title I funds are translated into additional local education spending, whereas grant-in-aid programs more generally tend to be substitutes for locally financed expenditures. Stephen M. Barro, "Federal Education Goals and Policy Instruments: An Assessment of the 'Strings' Attached to Categorical Grants in Education," in *The Federal Interest in Financing Schooling,* ed. Michael Timpane (Cambridge, Mass.: Ballinger, 1978), p. 237.

34. Richard P. Nathan, Allen D. Manvel, and Susannah E. Calkins, *Monitoring Revenue Sharing* (Washington, D.C.: Brookings Institution, 1975), p. 100.

35. Ibid., p. 109.

36. Gary Orfield, "Desegregation of Black and Hispanic Students from 1968 to 1980" (Washington, D.C.: Joint Center for Political Studies, 1982), p. 15.